PUBS IN BRITAIN

– seeing is believing –

Title Number 1. First edition.

WRITTEN & PUBLISHED BY

STRANGEST BOOKS

Published in England by Strangest Books (http://www.strangestbooks.co.uk).
Text, design and complete contents copyright, 2002, is the property of
Strangest Books in accordance with the Copyright, Designs and Patents Act 1988.

ISBN 0 9543202 0 4

ACKNOWLEDGEMENTS

Thanks are given to those people who have kindly provided some of the photographs for
inclusion in this book. These photographs are reproduced with the permission of the
relevant copyright holders.

This book is the result of extensive research and the entries contained herein are
inserted at the sole discretion of the publishers. This does not indicate a preference over
establishments not included. The publishers receive no payments or inducements for
inclusion in this book.

FRONT COVER PICTURES

top left - Widow's Son - page 21
top centre - Horse & Jockey - page 80
top right - The Crooked House - page 13
middle left - Lucky Jims - page 29
middle centre - Somerset House - page 19
middle right - Ye Olde Royal Oak - page 18
bottom left - Ben Crouch Tavern - page 92
bottom centre - The Union Inn - page 84
bottom right - Nut Tree - page 68

foreword

Most of us can clearly remember a time when we saw or read about something that was so strange or unusual it made us gasp in wonder, or even sent a cold chill through our body.

The Strangest series of Books has the very best compilations of all that is weird, amazing and bizarre in Britain today and will open up a wonderland of curiosities for you to discover, most of which you probably never knew existed.

Each of the books in our series covers a chosen subject and will provide you with a thoroughly entertaining read. There are fascinating, mysterious, and very often unbelievable places and things to be seen in Britain. Some are so unusual that only a visit to actually see for yourself will suffice, or you can simply experience an unforgettable bedtime read - and then amaze your friends and colleagues with some of the startling facts.

Sure to provide readers with as much pleasure as they did for the researchers, the Strangest series of Books can be purchased or ordered from all good book stores and high street retailers. Information on how to order direct can be found on page 96.

'Outside of a dog,

a book is a man's best friend.

Inside of a dog, it's too dark to read.'

- Groucho Marx

about this book

With well over 60,000 to choose from, the abundance and diversity of pubs in Britain is truly superb and it is little wonder that in this respect we are envied worldwide.

As most people are fascinated by the unusual, this book, the Strangest Pubs in Britain, is dedicated to providing readers with tales of the weirdest and wackiest pubs there are. Read all about the amazing Crooked House where your glass slides up the table, or the pub where you play skittles with a block of cheese! Then there is the story behind the strange collection of shrivelled mouldy buns, or how would you like to be served your drink by a robot?

Find out where the smallest, oldest and most remote pubs are, and where you can berth your canal boat at the bar! The World Black Pudding throwing championships, a door made with human skin, a pub with its own mortuary, mummified hands, the amazing Pack of Cards, - even the World Toe-Wrestling championships. Over 160 of the strangest pubs you are ever likely to find - all here in a book you will want to read again and again.

1 Northumberland
2 Tyne & Wear
3 Cumbria
4 Durham
5 Cleveland
6 Lancashire
   & Manchester
7 Yorkshire
8 Humberside
9 Merseyside
10 Cheshire
11 Derbyshire
12 Nottinghamshire
13 Lincolnshire
14 Shropshire
15 Staffordshire
16 Leicestershire
17 Herefordshire
18 Worcestershire

19 West Midlands
20 Warwickshire
21 Northamptonshire
22 Cambridgeshire
23 Norfolk
24 Gloucestershire
25 Oxfordshire
26 Buckinghamshire
27 Bedfordshire
28 Hertfordshire
29 Suffolk
30 Essex
31 Somerset & Bristol
32 Wiltshire
33 Berkshire
34 London
35 Cornwall
36 Devon
37 Dorset
38 Hampshire
39 Isle of Wight
40 Surrey
41 Sussex
42 Kent

Scotland

Wales

This map is intended as a guide only and is not fully representative of any features or to scale.

alphabetical index of entries

LONDON

MERSEYSIDE

NORFOLK

NORTHAMPTONSHIRE

NORTHUMBERLAND

NOTTINGHAMSHIRE

OXFORDSHIRE

WALES . . . *continued*

WEST MIDLANDS

WILTSHIRE

WORCESTERSHIRE

YORKSHIRE

The optical extravaganza of The Crooked House
where seeing puts a different slant on things.

THE CROOKED HOUSE
Coppice Mill, Himley,
near Dudley, Staffordshire

This typical 'black country' pub was built as a farmhouse in 1765 and is one of the country's best public house attractions - as a pub that really is crooked. It was originally known as 'The Glynne Arms' as it was named after Sir Stephen Glynne on whose estate the pub stood.

The pub is now 4ft lower on one side than on the other due to subsidence from the effects of coal mining during the 1800's, and it is heavily supported with buttresses and girders.

The amazing angle that the pub sits at has to be seen to be believed. In fact The Crooked House is one huge optical illusion where curtains hang away from the window frames, marbles roll uphill on the wall beading, and drinks slide slowly 'up table'. It is also allegedly haunted.

shoe deposits & snail racing

THE FROG & TOAD
**38 Burnt Oak Terrace,
Gillingham, Kent**

Popular and worth visiting for more than one unusual reason The Frog & Toad pub in Gillingham sells a huge range of Belgian beers, but it is one type in particular that will leave you 'legless', or more specifically 'shoeless'!

The tradition in Belgium if you want to buy the 8% 'Kwak' ale is that you leave one of your shoes as a deposit - to prevent souvenir hunters running off with the elaborate glass and wooden frame it is served in. The glass is shaped like a miniature 'yard of ale' and as it will not rest on the counter it is supported in an ornamental wooden frame, complete with handle, with the combination costing about £5 each to manufacture.

The Frog & Toad have taken the idea one step further and have six ropes behind the bar which run over the ceiling of the bar to the customers side and are attached to wire baskets. The customer - by now bemused - is asked to deposit his shoe in the basket which is in turn hoisted up to the ceiling, remaining there until the return of the glass and frame.

Unscrupulous patrons who deposit a shoe that is obviously on its last legs will be politely requested to stick a £5 note inside as an added security!

Big attractive thermal slipper socks are offered to customers who suffer from 'cold feet' and these are washed together with the bar towels, which gives a whole new meaning to smelly feet.

Equally wacky is the inspirational idea of snail racing, and the team who were responsible for the Guinness television advert hosted one such event at The Frog & Toad. It was a huge success, has been held again, and looks set to become the annual World Championships.

There were 10 snails in each race all of which had a number attached to their shell. Racing on a damp cloth from a small inner circle to a larger outer circle, the first across the outside line was the winner.

Customers backed their favourite snail and, thoughtfully, all profits were donated to good causes.

As a pub which evidently takes great pride in offering its customers variety, albeit of a mildly eccentric nature, another idea set to become a permanent feature is 'suitcase sales'. Derived from ever popular car boot sales this is strictly suitcases only and is held on Sundays, weather permitting, in the garden of this twice winner of the Camra Pub of the Year award.

Snails and slugs are gastropods which make up the largest class of molluscs with over 60,000 species. Snails move about by sliding on their single foot which has a specialised gland to secrete mucus. This lubricates the path over which the snails crawl. Freshwater snails and land snails have always been eaten by people and they are a delicacy in many countries.

A previous Guinness Gastropod Championship held in central London featured an attempt to break the world 13 inch sprinting record which was held by 'Archie' at an incredible 2 minutes and 20 seconds. This equates to a speed of 0.0085 kilometres per hour although it is said that snails have been measured at speeds of 0.048 kilometres per hour. It has also been recorded that a common garden snail averages 0.03 miles per hour.

Depositing a shoe for 'Kwak' ale and (below) not quite a sprint finish with snail racing.

roman bath

THE ROMAN BATH
St.Sampson's Square, York, Yorkshire

Hidden away for 2,000 years, the famous well preserved Roman Bath in the basement of this pub is now open to the public. Splendidly displayed and illuminated, visitors can enjoy the experience from a specially constructed viewing platform.

The pub itself also has superb depictions of Roman times running the length of its walls and no visit to York, one of the most important Roman historical cities in the country, would be complete without a visit to The Roman Bath.

THE CHURCH HOUSE INN
Harberton, Totnes, Devon

Once a Chantry House for monks, the lattice glass on the back wall of The Church House Inn is over 700 years old and is the earliest example of non-ecclesiastical glass in the country.

CRIDFORD INN
Trusham, Newton Abbot, Devon

The transept window in the bar of this historic inn is said to be the oldest domestic window in Britain.

Viewing platform at the Roman Bath.

Depicting Roman life and (below) close up view of Roman bath.

toe wrestling

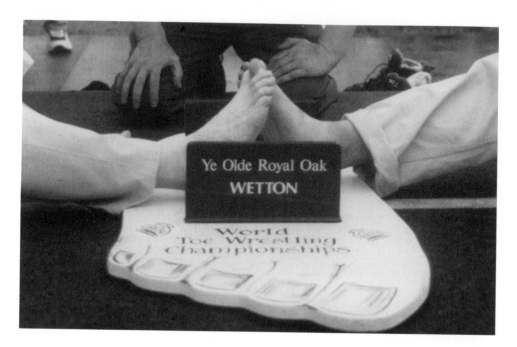

The action begins and (right) Ralf Little from television's 'Royle Family' gets to grips.

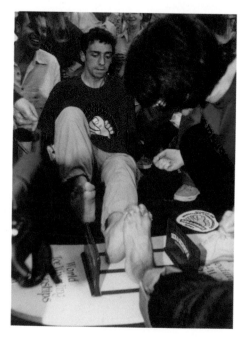

YE OLDE ROYAL OAK
Wetton Village, near Ashbourne, Derbyshire

Would all enthusiasts of Toe Wrestling please note that Ye Olde Royal Oak is the international centre of this sport. Unbelievably true, the official world championships are held here every summer.

At other times of the year the locals will be pleased to run through the rules and tactics of the sport perhaps over a pint of 'Anklecracker', an ale brewed especially to celebrate the importance of this annual event.

SOMERSET HOUSE
121 Enville Street, Stourbridge, West Midlands

Who would have believed it? The subject of various television, radio and newspaper reports, Somerset House - an unassuming West Midlands local - hit the headlines as a pub where you can park your pint unsupported on its walls! With a sceptical mind (and a lunchtime thirst) we went along to investigate, and came away as bemused as the German camera crew who had preceded us. The phenomenon has been probed by scientists who arrived at the conclusion that the wallpaper glue was responsible. Their assumption is based on a suspicion that a combination of glue, old tobacco smoke and grime is enough to hold a full pint against the wall, sometimes for a day or more, although they admit it is very odd.

Regulars at Somerset House are not convinced however and believe the walls are magic, whilst others insist the pub is haunted. Spookily enough coffins used to be assembled on this land just out the back and tales abound of mysterious happenings over the years.

What is beyond dispute is the fact that the photograph below was taken by our own photographer and shows his pint suspended unaided from the wall of the pub. Minutes later it was quaffed, and very welcome it was too!

Old buns and fresh buns at the Widow's Son in East London.

WIDOW'S SON
75 Devon's Road, Bow, London E3

A sad tale accompanies the curiously named Widow's Son in East London. Prior to it becoming a pub a poor widow lived in a cottage on this site about 200 years ago. Her only son was a sailor and as he was due to return home from sea one Good Friday his mother baked him some hot-cross buns. Unfortunately he never returned home and nothing was heard of him again, but his mother continued to have a new bun waiting for him every Good Friday thereafter - which was subsequently added to the buns she had kept from previous years. When she died the buns were discovered hanging from a beam in her cottage which became known to locals as 'Bun House' and, although the cottage was eventually replaced by a pub around 1848, this delightful story and tradition was continued by successive landlords.

Every Good Friday a Royal Navy sailor arrives to present a new bun which is added to the mouldy shrunken collection that hangs over the bar, and today, sailors from all parts of the country call in from time to time to pay their respects to the widow - in addition to having a good time at this plain and unassuming East London pub.

THE BELL INN
High Road, Horndon-On-The-Hill, Stanford-Le-Hope, Essex

A similar although not a tragic story concerns the attractive timber beamed bar at the medieval 15th century Bell Inn in Essex. They too have an odd collection of hot cross buns hanging from their heavy beams. The story here is that the pub was taken over on Good Friday of 1903 by Jack Turnell who celebrated the occasion by hanging a hot cross bun from the timbers.

The tradition has been kept going ever since and even during the war when food was scarce a concrete bun was hung instead! Nowadays the oldest person available at the time has the honour of hanging the annual bun every Easter at The Bell Inn.

THE EAGLE BAR & BAKERY
125 Gloucester Road, Brighton, Sussex

This is the only pub in Britain with a fully working bakery on the premises and is believed to be the first of its kind in the world. The open bakery can be found in one corner of the bar and customers at the pub can watch the baker at work. Anything baked here can be bought as a take-away including traditional loaves such as farmhouse or granary, or delicious imaginative bakes like beer flavoured or walnut. There is of course a lot more to choose from.

The bakery produce is best enjoyed with a meal in the dining room above, and the pub also supplies many other pubs and businesses in the locality with bread. This must be one of very few pubs where the staff start work at 5am!

Observational hive and (below) outdoor hives at the amazing Honeybee Inn.

900 years of honey

No need to get a bee in your bonnet here; there's plenty of honey for all.

HONEYBEE INN
Doverdale Lane, Doverdale, Droitwich Spa, Worcestershire

Situated in a spectacular rolling countryside setting, the amazing Honeybee Inn is Britain's only honey farm pub where honey is actually produced on the premises - and has been for at least 900 years.

A plethora of honey-making memorabilia from centuries past adorns this huge and delightfully appointed pub which is sure to enthral all the family.

Honeycomb ale is always available in addition to a menu that offers many delicious dishes made with all types of honey. The interior workshop offers the chance to actually see the honey extraction process taking place.

A shop inside the inn has a huge range of honey and related items available for purchase.

Dozens of large hives are scattered around the outside of the inn with at least a dozen or more active at any one time, mostly near the pool at the bottom of the hill.

It is said that even today the local inhabitants of Doverdale still smear their newly born children with Doverdale Honey in a ritual which predates Christianity. The health giving and medical qualities are said to prove its worth.

most notorious pub

LORD NELSON
Walsingham Road, Burnham Thorpe, King's Lynn, Norfolk

This pub is over 300 years old and is located in the village where Lord Horatio Nelson was born. Highly unusual is the fact that there is no bar here, and never has been! Long before licensing laws came into effect most inns did not have bar areas, and when almost all followed suit by providing a serving bar years later, the Lord Nelson did not. It still serves traditional real ales and provides all that you would expect from a typical pub - with the exception that table service is provided and the drinks are brought in from a room at the back.

THE GREYHOUND INN
Tinsley Green, Crawley, Sussex

Childhood memories will come flooding back if you visit The Greyhound Inn on a Good Friday when they play host to the World Marbles Championships. It has been held here since at least the 1930's but is believed to have been a lot longer than that.
The main marble ring is on the pub car park with 4 further rings located in the gardens. Visitors travel from all corners of the world to participate.

THE HORSESHOE BAR
17 Drury Street, Glasgow, Scotland

The Horseshoe bar dates from around 1886 and is quite possibly the busiest pub in Scotland. It is believed to have the longest continual island bar in Europe at 114ft in length!

GEORGE & DRAGON
High Street, Cley-next-the-Sea, Norfolk

Dedicated to bird-watching of the feathered kind, the George & Dragon is the ideal place for 'twitchers' to pursue their hobby. Cley Marshes Nature Reserve has resident herons, wagtails, hawks, grebes and woodpeckers - in addition to visiting cormorants, puffins and razorbills, etc.
This imposing building has its own 'hide' where watchers can observe some of the rare species. One bedroom/hide room can be reserved (with binoculars supplied free of charge), and a separate room is for general observation by twitchers.
A 'Bird Bible' (or diary) is located on a lectern and contains many illustrations by famous bird watchers. It is updated on a daily basis and provides watchers with a wealth of information.

THE BLIND BEGGAR
337 Whitechapel Road, Spitalfields, London E1

Located near where the notorious Jack the Ripper murder attrocities occurred The Blind Beggar could possibly be described as Britain's most notorious pub. Although now a very pleasant establishment, on March 8th of 1966 George Cornell of the infamous Richardson gang was drinking in The Blind Beggar when Ronald Kray, one of the Kray twins, walked into the bar and shot him dead through the head.

gigantic tree in pub

WAXY O'CONNORS
14-16 Rupert Street,
London W1

The labyrinth of individually designed interconnecting rooms, bars and alcoves at Waxy O'Connors makes this the drinking experience of a lifetime. Gothic, Celtic, and awe-inspiring are words that readily spring to mind when attempting to describe this 9,000 square foot pub.

Entering at street level you then descend to other levels, and the many areas include the Cottage Room, the spectacular Church Bar complete with wood carvings, pulpit, confessional box and gargoyles, and the Tree Room - which features a massive 250 year old beech tree from the Midlands in Ireland, 'growing' from floor to ceiling through 2 storeys. A church from Ireland was actually taken down, transported here, and rebuilt.

Wherever you sit or stand at Waxy O'Connors there is a stunning feature to be admired and the lower level Dargle restaurant is no exception.

Enormous Irish beech tree growing through 2 storeys of Waxy O'Connors.

skittles played with cheese

GEORGE & DRAGON INN
High Street, Potterne, near Devizes, Wiltshire

The village of Potterne is mentioned in the Domesday Book, and at the George & Dragon Inn there is a tunnel leading to a pub in the next village.
It is known that this tunnel was used by Oliver Cromwell.

A unique .22 shooting gallery is housed within the pub, believed to be the only one located in a pub in the world, and regular competitions are held here every Thursday evening. Marksmen shoot along a metal tube from a hatch into the target area housed in an adjacent small building. New participants are always welcome and frequent open nights are held.

Incredibly, the whole thing was started here over 100 years ago in 1906 by a member of royalty.

THE GOLF BAR
Tithebar Street, Liverpool, Merseyside

This sports bar is located on the edge of the city centre in a business district. Golfing enthusiasts will find 2 golf simulators here in addition to other sporting attractions - and a professional golfer is on hand to offer tuition!

FREEMASONS ARMS
32 Downshire Hill, Hampstead, London NW3

Visitors to this attractive Regency style building will note a 'pell mell' court which has survived from the original pub - which was demolished after being found to be unsafe during extension work. The ancient game involved rolling a big wooden ball through iron hoops and was a form of croquet, but without the mallet.

There is also a London Skittle alley here in the Freemasons Arms cellar. The forerunner of tenpin bowling, it is played with 9 pins and involves throwing (not rolling) a cheese down a 21ft alley at the pins! The game is still played here on a regular basis.

LIFEBOAT INN
Ship Lane, Thornham, Norfolk

The Lifeboat Inn is a 16th century smugglers inn and has an ancient and quite uncommon game called 'penny-in-the-hole'. Set into a high backed wooden settle, players have to throw or pitch 13 old coins against a backdrop of lead into a hole in the seat. It is said that George III outlawed the game, although it is still played today.

As winners are extremely rare it would appear that the landlord can offer successful participants (apparently with little risk) a gallon of whisky as a prize. All 13 coins have to fall into the hole so the odds are stacked against the 'lobber'. Perhaps its better to try your luck at another old game called 'shove ha'penny', which the Lifeboat Inn also plays.

door made with human skin

THE HATCHET INN
27 Frogmore Street, Bristol

Once the haunt of notorious highwaymen, The Hatchet Inn is Bristol's oldest public house and was established in 1606. The 300 year old main door of the pub is said to have layers of human skin under the tar and many large offers have been made for it, but all declined.

A cockfighting ring and a boxing ring have been here, and bare knuckle fights involving 'All England Champions' attracted enormous purses in days gone by.

The Hatchet Inn and (left) the 300 year old front door of the pub, reputed to have layers of human skin under the tar coating.

launder while you drink

THE LAUNDROMATIC SUPERPUB
22 Caledonia Street, Liverpool, Merseyside

You could be forgiven for thinking you had mistakenly entered a wrong door when walking into this pub as what confronts you is an in-house launderette!

Incredible but true, there are coin operated launderette style washing machines and tumble dryers (installed in November 2000) which enables drinkers to wash their bedding or smalls without leaving the comfort of the pub.

The brainchild arose as a result of the burgeoning student population in the area. There are about 5,000 residential students within a 5 minute walking distance - helping to make The Laundromatic Superpub a runaway success.

The pub has also converted old domestic washing machines into fish tanks plus it offers patrons free use of the internet.

MARINE
61 Seaside, Eastbourne, Sussex

The Marine pub will appeal greatly to literary enthusiasts as there is a small lending library here where you can borrow books in exactly the same way you would at a normal library. There are over 200 books to choose from and it is all operated on a trust and honesty basis. The idea arose as a result of the local council library closing its doors in 1999.

THE CAT'S BACK
86 Point Pleasant, London SW18

This tiny pub has been described as 'eccentric with eccentric staff', and not without justification. It resembles a curiosity shop with a bar where visitors can admire - or ponder - the numerous odd and weird souvenirs that have been accrued here. African and Pacific island paintings, Indian chairs, and a host of bric-a-brac jostle for space in a myriad of fascinating clutter.

The pub is named after a cat who disappeared but later returned.

THE ARCTIC BAR
3-5 New Entry, Dundee, Scotland

This is one of the oldest pubs in the area and the name 'Arctic Bar' is believed to have originated from the whalers who used to call in and collect their wages at the bar. In keeping with its name, one of the most prominenet features is a depiction in the floor of the bar showing a polar bear on top of an iceberg.

There are also 6 doors in the bar area that each have coffin shaped windows, probably installed in memory of 6 local whalers who were lost at sea. Whaling once formed a major part of the economy in this part of Scotland and old unused whaling stations can still be seen today.

miniature beer pump televisions

Action all the way at Lucky Jims.

LUCKY JIMS
27-29 Leigh Road, Eastleigh, Hampshire

Never miss a second of the sporting action at Lucky Jims in Eastleigh, said to be the first pub in the world to install miniature 4 inch (10 centimetre) monitors on the beer pump 'T-bars'.

They display all the sporting action that is playing on the large screens around the pub and can also be put to use for advertising purposes, and to promote special future events to be held at the pub.

It certainly makes watching sporting events that much more attractive as you can catch all the action as you wait to be served your drink.

pub with no name

THE WHITE HORSE
Priors Dean, near Petersfield, Hampshire

Countryside pub enthusiasts will be pleased to visit The White Horse - if they can find it that is, as the pub is isolated in the middle of a field and has no name sign! It was constructed in 1620 and used to serve an old road but when that road was straightened to afford a more direct route, The White Horse found itself stranded in the middle of a field. The sign at the old crossroads indicating the way to the pub was taken down and never replaced, and as it is believed the pub has never had its own sign it has since become known as 'the Pub With No Name'.

Once discovered this is a pub not easily forgotten as the atmosphere and interior are truly superb. The well known poet Edward Thomas has a wood carving on the wall to commemorate him as his first published poem was about The White Horse.

This impressive white painted building has excellent views of the surrounding South Downs and remains an oddity - by virtue of its 'Pub With No Name' status - to this very day.

curious village of crosses

TREVOR ARMS HOTEL
Marford Village, Wrexham, Clwyd, North Wales

Marford is an amazing village full of buildings that ooze character and the odd thing is that most of the buildings, including The Trevor Arms Hotel which dates back to the early 1800's, feature a cross or crosses which are intended to ward off evil spirits. In fact The Trevor Arms Hotel has 4 or 5 of these set into its structure.

The story relates that following a battle in Paris between Catholics and Protestants in the late 1700's, which the Catholics won, the Protestants made their escape up the River Seine and eventually, via the River Dee, landed at Ecclestone Ferry nearby.

Marford Village is built in a Dutch style, with a place in Holland believed to be identical. There is little doubt that the buildings and their unusual architecture - with even more striking windows and strange crosses - are the work of these Europeans.

An unusual dwelling, below, in the village of Marford.

The rear of the Trevor Arms Hotel, above, with crosses hewn in the stonework.

eternal fires

THE SALTERSGATE INN
Saltersgate, Pickering, Yorkshire

Having a very picturesque setting on the North Yorkshire Moors, this historic inn is over 400 years old. Following the famous voyage by Captain Cook an unofficial voyage to follow it was planned here by Jack Lannerman.

Visitors will be amazed to know that the fire that crackles away in the cast iron range at The Saltersgate Inn has been doing so perpetually for over 200 years. You can read of the Saltersgate Inn Legend here that tells you the full story of this 'eternal fire'.

It is said that the devil himself will plague all the locality should the fire ever be allowed to go out.

WARREN HOUSE INN
Postbridge, Devon

The Warren House Inn has a fireplace at either end of its cosy bar, one of which has been kept continually alight since it was built in 1845. Prior to that the pub was located on the other side of the road and it is believed that a fire was also lit permanently there for at least another 150 years! The reason behind this would have been for the benefit of tin miners working in the area, with peat being the traditional fuel. Although those days are long gone the tradition of keeping the fire alight lives on. Incidentally, this is also one of the highest pubs in England (1,545ft) and has no mains electricity or water!

WHITE CROSS HOTEL
Water Lane, Riverside, Richmond, Surrey

The White Cross Hotel is located on the site of the Observant Friars - a white cross being their insignia. As the River Thames floods regularly here a sign on the wall reads 'entrance at high tide', but the pub is perhaps better known as having fires beneath windows!

There were originally 3 of these fires positioned directly under windows although of the 2 in the flat above, one is now bricked up. The other is located in the bar. It is assumed that views of the river were wanted whilst sitting by a fire and hence the reason for this very rare arrangement.

BLACK BULL INN
Hall Lane, Mawdesley, Ormskirk, Merseyside

A spring water well, 40ft deep, lies under the floor of the Black Bull Inn. For the aforementioned fires this pub has an adequate instrument - an original black 16lb poker about 4'6" long, and one of the biggest in the country. A quotation says of the poker: 'surely big enough to stoke and poke the fires of hell'.

built like a pack of cards

PACK O'CARDS
High Street, Combe Martin, Devon

A remarkable pub which is a magnet for tourists, this was built by the village squire in 1690 as a tribute to 'lady luck' with the winnings from a card game.

Constructed to resemble a deck of cards, it was built on a plot of land measuring 52ft x 52ft, has 4 floors (representing the number of suits in a pack), 13 doors on every floor and 13 fireplaces (number of cards in a suit), 52 stairs (number of cards in a pack), and prior to window tax the panes of glass in all the windows added up to the total of the numbered cards in a pack!

chicken races & ufo's

THE BARLEY MOW
The Dale, Bonsall, Matlock, Derbyshire

For more than 10 years The Barley Mow at Bonsall has held its world famous 'Chicken Races'. On the first Saturday in August a 20 metre marked track on the car park is transformed into a feather-flying battle of the fittest hens around. There have been rumours that hen racing has been held in the area for decades and The Barley Mow is said to be carrying on that tradition.

Strict rules are in place here - birds must start with their feet on the ground (no air launched hens allowed), cockerels and dogs are barred for the day, and violence is strictly prohibited as hen-pecking can lead to a suspension!

The event is extremely popular with large crowds always in attendance to witness this 'egg'-straordinary annual spectacle.

The village of Bonsall has made the headlines many times regarding numerous mysterious UFO sightings in the area. Around 20 sightings were reported during one month alone including one by a lady that was actually recorded on camcorder. It was said in the local newspaper that she was paid a figure of £20,000 by a television company for exclusive rights to the footage which showed an unidentified craft hovering over fields near her home.

The area in general is a hotbed for UFO sightings and a constant stream of visitors from all over the country call in at The Barley Mow public house to join the landlord's tours - in the hope of witnessing an extraterrestrial occurrence themselves.

Many villagers are said to have experienced these unexplained sightings but most are reluctant to talk about them. The pub landlord patiently and frequently spends time with visitors to The Barley Mow discussing the sightings and informing them of the best reported locations to visit.

There is no doubt that something is afoot at Bonsall and it is hoped that either further investigations, or future irrefutable evidence, may yet reveal that we are not alone!

THE STAR INN
23 The Vineyards, off The Paragon, Bath, Somerset

An irregular addition to the fixtures and fittings of The Star Inn is a lift that is used to transport barrels through the trap-door of the cellar. The pub is a unique example of a Gaskell & Chambers fitted pub with many original features remaining such as numbered rooms, which the Licensing Laws required at the time to illustrate their purpose.

There is a long narrow bench in the bar known as 'death row'. The reason for this peculiar name is not known, but equally peculiar is the odd yet quaint tradition that has been in place for over 100 years - the complimentary snuff that is found on the ledge above the wall panelling. There are over 10 different kinds available for patrons use.

One of the oldest inns to be found in the area, The Star Inn is sure to rekindle memories of yesteryear.

THE LITTLE DRY DOCK
Windmill End, Netherton, near Dudley, West Midlands

Built as a barge-station for boats going up the Netherton Tunnel to New Street Station, this was turned into a pub shortly after the war - with a complete narrowboat still inside which is now actually the bar! The pub is full of barge memorabilia and is located below an impressive junction of the canal network.

Opposing views of a bar that is actually a barge.

waiting for a train

TAFARN SINC PRESELI
**Preseli, Rosebush,
Clunderwen, Sir Benfro,
West Wales**

Constructed in 1876 when the railway was opened from Clunderwen to Rosebush, this was originally built and operated as an hotel under the name of the 'Precelly Hotel'. In 1992, in a bad state of repair, it was closed by the brewery and was subsequently bought by locals. Refurbished and re-named the 'Tafarn Sinc Preseli' it is now more like a home than a pub, but this big zinc shed has traditional old world charm and values that everyone will appreciate.

Salt-cured hams hang from the beams, and a dresser, settles and lots of memorabilia jostle for space. Predominantly Welsh speaking here, visitors can enjoy panoramic breathtaking views all around - this is the highest licensed pub in Pembrokeshire.

No visit to the Tafarn Sinc Preseli would be complete without seeing the amazing reconditioned railway halt and platform here that is complete with life size dummies and sound effects.

bog-snorkelling championships

THE NEUADD ARMS HOTEL
Llanwrtyd Wells, Powys, Mid Wales

Whether it is a beer festival, a real ale 'wobble walk', or a man versus horse marathon (over a mountain), chances are that an event will be taking place when you visit The Neuadd Arms Hotel. The most bizarre of all is the World Bog-Snorkelling Championships that are held here each August. For those with raised eyebrows who are unfamiliar with this most peculiar event, bog-snorkelling involves being underwater in a 60ft specially excavated trench in a local bog and travelling along the bottom of the trench to a post which is inserted at the other end - and then back again!

THE LAMB OF RHOS
Rhos, Llangeler, Carmarthenshire, West Wales

This flagstone floored country inn has its own jail which is now used as a childrens playroom, and the unusual carved 'seat to nowhere' located in an arch in the bar. 'Nowhere or Now Here' is the inscription for it and these words are the beginning of a poem which was written by a local.

OLDE BULLS HEAD
Castle Street, Beaumaris, Anglesey, North Wales

Amongst the many notable artefacts on display at the Olde Bulls Head in Beaumaris is the town's old ducking stool and some fearsome looking cutlasses. The pub however is most famous for the gigantic courtyard door which is the largest single-hinged door in Britain.

THE SCOTSMAN PACK INN
School Lane, Hathersage, Hope Valley, Derbyshire

'Little John' was a giant whose body now lies in a grave at a Hathersage graveyard. A chair which was specially constructed for him can be seen at The scotsman Pack Inn. It is affectionately known as 'Little John's Chair' and was won in a wager by a Major John J. Lewis of the Manchester Regiment, from Lieutenant A. Sunderland of the Royal Tank Regiment in 1950.
   It is known that the chair was at the pub during the 1920's and 1930's, although it then went missing for a while, but was presented back to the pub by a Mrs M. Lucas in 1960. The immense chair is a rare sight indeed.

THE MALTINGS
Tanners Moat, York, Yorkshire

The front of the bar and the entire ceiling of The Maltings is completely made from doors!

mummified hand

HAUNCH OF VENISON
Salisbury, Wiltshire

This was constructed as the church house for nearby St.Thomas's.
In addition to a 600 year old fireplace this ancient old building has a glass covered slit in the wall behind which is a smoke preserved, mummified hand of a most unfortunate 18th century card player!

*Hand of an ill-fated
18th century card player at the
Haunch of Venison.*

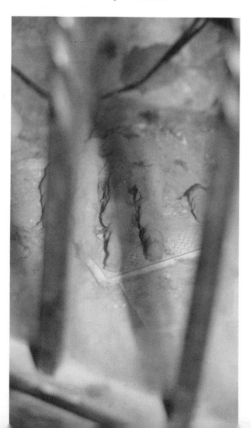

OXENHAM ARMS
South Zeal, Okehampton, Devon

First licensed in 1477, Charles Dickens wrote a lot of the Pickwick Papers at this establishment. The pub has matured amidst the remains of a Norman monastery which was constructed here to fend off the alleged power of a neolithic standing stone. This stone can be viewed here as it forms part of the wall in one of the rooms. There is also a further 20ft or so of it below ground.

THREE STAGS HEADS
Wardlow, Derbyshire

This small unpretentious stone cottage pub has a tiny flagstoned parlour. The plates are home-made here in addition to the food, as the barn is in use as a pottery workshop! Another curiosity is the petrified cat in a glass case which was found during refurbishments. It had evidently been bricked up alive centuries ago and could have been the result of a macabre practice amongst local lead miners

TAN HILL INN
Richmond, Tan Hill, Yorkshire

This isolated old stone pub is Britain's highest at 1,732ft above sea level. It is located on the border of North Yorkshire and Durham - also close to the border with Cumbria - and often becomes snowbound during winter.

smallest pubs

THE LAKESIDE INN
**Marine Lake, Promenade,
Southport, Merseyside**

Once a private sailing club this is thought by many to be the smallest pub in Britain. The measurements are just 22ft x 16ft and approximately 15ft high. Fine views over the Marine Lake can be had here, and in case you are wondering, the handles that are halfway down the doors in the gents toilets were installed for the 7 dwarfs - who visited the pub after appearing at the nearby Southport Theatre!

THE NUTSHELL
**1 The Traverse,
Bury St.Edmunds, Suffolk**

Also widely acclaimed to be the tiniest of them all is The Nutshell that comes in at 15ft x 7ft 6in. Miniscule by any standards, it has to be said that The Nutshell is built on 3 floors and the measurements relate only to the ground floor. This amazing pub also boasts a mini fruit machine and jukebox, the smallest dart board and snooker table, and a wee Grandfather clock. Look out also for a 3 legged chicken, a left leg and a mummified cat and mouse!

DOVE PUBLIC HOUSE
19 Upper Mall, London W6

Many celebrity customers have been past visitors to the Dove Public House, and James Thomson (who wrote 'Rule Britannia') lodged and died here. Who knows where they all sat as the pub has the smallest bar in Britain - only 4ft 2in x 7ft 10in.

THE JOHN'S CROSS
**Battle Road,
near Robertsbridge, Sussex**

The John's Cross Inn was previously used as a marshalling point for Crusaders and has also seen duty as a recruiting office during the Napoleonic Wars. On a more up to date note the pub boasts very impressive floral displays outside and has been quoted in one gardening magazine as the 'hanging gardens of John's Cross'.

Another claim to fame here is that this is the only pub sign company in Britain actually situated on licensed premises (the studio is located at the back of the pub).

Visitors to this delightful pub may care to dine in either the bar or the designated dining room, which still houses an original bread oven. It is said to be the smallest dining room of any pub in the country at a measured size of 6ft 1in x 6ft 3in

THE MINERVA
**Nelson Street,
Hull, Humberside**

Built in 1831 on land reclaimed from the River Humber, The Minerva is an assortment of small rooms with one in particular being very, very small. The room in question is barely 4ft x 4ft and would be better described as a 'snug'. More than 2 people and it is standing room only here in what is probably the smallest room open to the public in any pub in the country.

heavens above

THE FARMHOUSE
St.Isidore's Road,
Grange Farm,
Kesgrave, Suffolk

The word of God is administered to pub-goers in this Suffolk village inn by a Reverend from the local All Saints Church. Parishioners have welcomed the idea which was started towards the end of 2001 and is now a regular monthly occurrence.

The first service was held in conjunction with a simultaneous service at the 900 year old All Saints Church - the service ending abruptly when the pub opened its doors at noon!

The vicar believes the services will help diminish the staid image that people have of them and all denominations in the parish believe it is a great idea.

The pub is now affectionately known as 'All Saints Farmhouse Community Pub'.

THE STAR INN
High Street, Alfriston,
near Polegate, Sussex

This pub was originally known as the 'Star of Bethlehem' when it was built and run as a hospice by monks from Battle Abbey. During the 1500's it was converted into an inn, and as the Roman Catholic associations of its name were frowned upon by Puritans, it was subsequently changed to 'Star'.

Numerous carved wooden figures look down from the outside of the pub and pay homage to its religious origins. It is believed that the exterior of The Star Inn is one of the best preserved of any pub in the country The hideous figurehead is said to have been salvaged from a Dutch ship that sank centuries ago.

The pub is also very striking internally and amongst many items is an old sanctuary post that people could use to gain protection by the church, from prosecution by the law.

THE RED LION
Llanafan Fawr, Builth Wells,
Powys, Mid Wales

It is believed that The Red Lion dates back at least 1,000 years - certainly to at least 1188 when a travelling monk known as 'Gerald of Wales' stayed at the inn whilst recruiting for Crusades. The present Red Lion dates from about 1472 although some of the original timbers are still clearly visible.

The remains of a 2,000 year old Celtic village can be seen, a yew tree that is at least 2,200 years old (authenticated) sits opposite, and old Llanafan churchyard (which was once a magnet for pilgrimages) contains the remains of many notable Welsh Bishops.

Today the pub, church and churchyard, retain many secrets. There are numerous tales of strange religious ceremonies and also witchcraft.

One gravestone states that a John Price was murdered in 1826 over a dispute regarding sheep rights, just behind the pub. It also names the murderer - and relatives of both families still live in Llanafan.

The Red Lion of today hosts the World Tippit Championships (an ancient game) and has also been home to the Welsh National Sheep Dog Championships.

the skull & the poltergeist

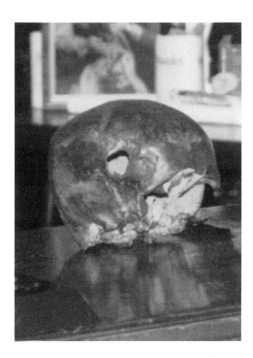

The 'George Skull'.

D. LAFFERTY & SON
41 Iron Gate, Derby, Derbyshire

Previously called The George and built around 1693 there are many strange tales surrounding this pub. Now called D. Lafferty & Son (although it is believed the pub may soon revert to its original name) this was once the most famous coaching inn in Derby.

The 'George Skull' on display in the pub is a female human skull that has a damaged cranium. It was discovered by workmen in a pit below the cellar floor together with animal bones and skulls, plus old shoes and pieces of leather. Forensic tests at Nottingham indicated a great age and the mystery is how, or why, only the skull and not the rest of the skeleton came to be in the pit.

As The George stands near the corner of Iron Gate (where blacksmiths traded) and Sadler Gate (where leather workers traded) which is the heart of Viking Derby, it can perhaps explain how the pieces of leather were discovered as it was usual for the leather makers to throw any off cuts into a pit after the hides had been stripped and tanned. An explanation for the animal bones and skulls may be that they were from animals killed for the leather makers. The enigma of the human skull and the damage to the side of it remains unsolved.

The pub is undoubtably haunted as on a few occasions a long haired man in a blue coat has been seen walking along the landing in the middle of the night. When followed down to the bar he has simply disappeared, although there was nowhere for him to go. Staff have reported many odd experiences since the building work and extension of the cellar has been completed including buckets being thrown, crockery moving by itself, pint pots smashed, and ghastly groans emanating from the cellar.

There is also said to be a ghost named Martha who frequently insists that her head (the 'George Skull') be taken from the bar and reburied.

As the mysteries surrounding the skull continues to baffle all who seek the answers we can only wonder - was she murdered and if so why? Where is the rest of her skeleton? Is she the ghostly presence behind all the strange happenings at the pub? What is known is that 2 murders have actually taken place in the adjoining alley!

discovering dna

EAGLE
Bene't Street, Cambridge, Cambridgeshire

This pub was once the headquarters of notorious swindler John Morlock who headed the Rutland Club in the 18th century, and more recently the famous Nobel Prize winning scientists Englishman Francis Crick and American James Watson who frequently imbibed at the pub. It was they who discovered the structure of DNA and on the last day of February of 1953 Francis Crick announced to all and sundry in the Eagle that he and Watson had unravelled the secret of life.

They had worked out that DNA is shaped like a twisted staircase - the double helix and the 2 strands of the helix consisted of very long strings of nucleotides. These in turn had sub-units referred to as A, T, G, and C (adenine, thymine, guanine, and cytosine) which when arranged into different combinations of 3 provide the meaningful instructions to our cells for our bodies to function correctly.

The Eagle is a busy town centre coaching inn which boasts medieval mullioned windows. The high ceiling has been untouched for many years so as not to cover up the many signatures worked in with candle smoke and lipstick of British and American airmen who served during the war.

PHILHARMONIC DINING ROOMS
36 Hope Street, Liverpool, Merseyside

This superb old Victorian establishment still retains a remarkably opulent feel about it and it is an architectural gem.

Originally opened as a gentlemans club it is evident that no expense was spared in both design and internal finishing. From the stained glass depictions and copper panels of musicians, to the intricate plasterwork and heavily carved partitions - it is little wonder that it was a previous winner of the 'Most ornate pub in Britain' award. There is of course a whole lot more to admire here not least the famous gents toilet. Original brass fittings, a riot of red marble and striking mosaics, and original 1890's Rouge Royale by Twyfords can all be seen. Spending a penny never felt so good!

THE CROWN INN
Ramsgate Road, Sarre, near Birchington, Kent

There has been an inn on this site since about 1500 and this Grade I Listed building previously played host to the many reunion dinners of the survivors of the famous Charge of the Light Brigade. It is known locally as the 'Cherry Brandy House' and the recipe for this drink was brought over by the Huguenots (French Protestants) who were fleeing from the religious persecutions of Louis XIV. It is believed that one of them bought the ale house at Sarre (which is now The Crown Inn) and started to produce the cherry brandy after being reminded of his family recipe when seeing fruit orchards in the area.

A requirement of subsequent licensees was that the liqueur be permanently available and today, the cherry brandy whose secret recipe is zealously guarded is sold exclusively at The Crown Inn and at nowhere else in the world!

THE CAPTAINS WIFE
Beach Road, Swanbridge, Sully, South Wales

The Captains Wife is a purpose built pub in a great location adjacent to Sully Bay which is part of the Bristol Channel. The pub overlooks Sully Island whilst further out in the Channel are the conservationist islands of Flat Holm and Steep Holme. Pubgoers who have had one too many are amongst those who often get stranded on Sully Island when the causeway they have walked across quickly becomes covered. The tides comes in twice as fast as it goes out with a two-way current that means opposing ends of your body can be pulled in different directions. A notice is posted on the island requesting that people stand in a particular spot so the coastguard can see them, such is the frequency of people becoming stranded here.

The island was once bought by an American women who intended (unsuccessfully) to make use of it as a nudist camp!

The Captains Wife with Sully Island in the distance and (below) the causeway leading out to the Island.

a pub below a pub

HALFWAY HOUSE
**24 Fleshmarket Close,
off the High Street,
Edinburgh, Scotland**

The Halfway House is a tiny
establishment located at the foot of
one of Edinburgh's atmospheric
alleyways and is one of the smallest
pubs in Scotland. It is actually a pub
below a pub as it is completely
situated under the main bar of the
adjoining pub on steep Fleshmarket
Close.

Once the scene of gambling exploits
of notorious rogue Deacon Brodie
(a nearby pub is named after him) the
Halfway House is full of character and
characters. The curiously named
'Fleshmarket Close' no doubt has many
a dark secret it could tell.

*Atmospheric
Fleshmarket Close,
Edinburgh, with a partial
view of one of Scotland's
smallest pubs - the
Halfway House.*

PUFF INN
St.Kilda, Outer Hebrides, Scotland

The archipeligo of St.Kilda found approximately 41 miles (66 kilometres) west of Benbecula in Scotland's Outer Hebrides consists of Hirta, Soay, Boreray and Dun, and they are collectively known as 'the islands at the edge of the world'. 'Kilda' is probably a corruption of the Norse word 'skildir' as there has never been a St. or Saint Kilda. There have been people on St.Kilda since Prehistoric times and stone tools discovered on Hirth indicate that Bronze Age travellers may have visited from the Western Isles up to 5,000 years ago. St.Kilda society existed virtually isolated from all others for well over 1,000 years until increasing contact with the mainland eventually brought about its downfall. Missionaries and tourists inevitably brought along with them the money orientated values of the mainland, in addition to diseases. In 1930 the islanders, who could no longer support themselves, were voluntarily evacuated. A small group emigrated to Australia, and even today a suburb of the city of Melbourne is called St.Kilda (there is also a St.Kilda in New Zealand).

In 1931 the islands were sold to a keen ornithologist, the 5th Marquess of Bute, who subsequently bequeathed them to the National Trust for Scotland in 1957. Due to its importance, in 1986 St.Kilda was designated a natural World Heritage Site. The exceptional cliffs which are the highest in Britain form the premier seabird breeding station in Europe, and the world's largest colony of gannets nests on Boreray. The St.Kildans used to eat seabirds as a major part of their diet with Puffin in particular being very popular.

Left on the islands is one of the most extensive groups of vernacular building remains to be found anywhere in Britain. The whole layout of the 19th century village remains can be seen to this day and there are over 1,400 stone cleitean (used for storing fuel and food) scattered all over the islands.

A small area of land on Hirta has been in use - on renewable 25 year leases - as a radar tracking station for the missile range located on Benbecula in the Outer Hebrides. St.Kilda attracts all sorts of people, in all kinds of weather, and in all types of craft.

Incredibly there is a pub on St.Kilda. The Puff Inn is the most remote pub in Britain being some 50 miles out in the Atlantic from Lewis in the Outer Hebrides. It is operated by Serco who run a lot of the Army facilities in Britain and caters for a resident population of 35 or so Army, conservation volunteers and wardens, sheep minders and visiting boats! It is a proper pub with liberal opening hours where anyone can get a drink, although being accessible only 3 months a year by boat, or at other times by helicoptor from Benbecula, you can hardly make it your new local.

THE OLD FORGE
Inverie, Knoydart, Mallaig, Inverness'shire, Scotland

The Old Forge is the most remote pub on mainland Britain, as confirmed by the Guinness Book of Records.

black pudding throwing

THE CORNER PIN
Stubbins, Ramsbottom, Lancashire

Black pudding is a delicious accompaniment to a traditional English breakfast but The Corner Pin pub has an altogether different use for it. On the second week in September each year they play host to the annual Black Pudding Throwing Championships where competitors make the trip from all over the world. The tradition of black pudding throwing is believed to date back as far as the War of the Roses and the event has been held at The Corner Pin pub, amazingly since 1862.

Around 100 - 230 people of all ages enter the event and contestants hurl the specially made 8 ounce puddings at giant Yorkshire puddings which are suspended on plates 20 ft off the ground. The aim is to knock as many Yorkshire puddings off as possible, and the black puddings are put into tights before being thrown to prevent them breaking up. The current world record is held by Ralph Hegginbothom who knocked an incredible 14 puddings off with a single shot in 1938. Other special award categories are held for 'original hurling technique' and 'throw a wobbler'.

THE STATION HOTEL
11 Park Street, Pickering, Yorkshire

A gravestone was discovered in the ceiling during renovations at The Station Hotel in 1961. It belonged to a lady called Elizabeth who reputedly haunts the pub to this day - and the gravestone is still in place in the ceiling!

OLD HOUSE INN
Upper Llangynwyd, near Maesteg, South Wales

The passing of one year into another is celebrated in parts of South Wales in a most unusual way. Of the many villages who are associated with the ancient Mari Lwyd (or 'Grey Mary') tradition, Llangynwyd is undoubtably the spiritual home. The Old House Inn has a Welsh sign with a painting of the Mari Lwyd which refers to this tradition and depicts Cynwyd Evans, who sadly died in 1997, clutching the reins of the Mari.

Customs involving animal skulls can be found all over the world but the Mari Lwyd is quite unique. Mari is the quaint name given to the skull itself (sometimes a real horse skull), which is decked in ribbons and has reins, false eyes and ears. This head is then carried around on top of a pole by someone who is disguised beneath a white sheet. The Mari Lwyd is then taken around the village from door to door - its jaws snapping open and shut - and accompanied by a motley crew of revellers who are all dressed up. Amidst much banter and requests for admission, the Mari and its party also seek permission to sing. Cwmni Dawns Werin Caerdydd (the City of Cardiff's official dance team) perform the tradition at the door of the Old House Inn every New Year's Eve in a dramatic fashion.

Dating back to 1147, this enchanting thatched pub is one of the oldest inns in Wales. This remarkable pub has even beaten Scotland's finest to the 'Whisky Pub of the Year' award recently.

biggest floating pub

CHARTERS
Town Bridge, Peterborough, Cambridgeshire

Believed to be the largest continental barge in the country and probably the biggest floating pub, this boat is the 'Leendert-R', a riveted iron Dutch barge built in 1907 and working until 1990 carrying up to 616 tonnes of cargo. Now known as Charters it was sailed across to England and up the River Nene to the Town Bridge, Peterborough and opened as a real ale bar in September 1991. At 176 ft long it is certainly a sight to behold.

FERRY BOAT
North Fambridge, Essex

A peculiarity of this unpretentious, over 500 years old weatherboarded pub is the fact that most of the building rests purely on a bed of reeds - which permit the old plaster and timber to move about in accordance with the local climate.

The impressive 'Leendert-R' Dutch barge, now Charters real ale bar.

cromwell's pewter legacy

THE FLEECE INN
The Cross, Bretforton, Evesham, Worcestershire

The Fleece Inn is a virtual living museum whose history can be traced back at least 1200 years. In 1848 it was converted from a working farm to an inn and mementos of the former owner, Miss Taplin, can be seen here. She bequeathed it to the nation and it is now owned by the National Trust.

Various rooms can be seen here such as 'The Dugout', but pride of place must be 'The Pewter Room' which houses a world famous collection of pewter that was reputedly abandoned by Cromwell.

GIN TRAP
The High Street, Ringstead, Norfolk

In keeping with its location the Gin Trap public house has an impressive collection of gin traps, a couple of which have been cleverly converted into electric candle effect wall lights.

A gin trap is a small animal trap and 'gin' is a diminutive of the word engine - and is therefore a device. Another fine collection here is the 100 plus chamberpots hanging from the old ceiling beams in the dining room.

World famous pewter collection abandoned by Cromwell.

THE BARGE INN
Honeystreet, near Pewsey, Wiltshire

The frequent new discoveries and overall enigma of crop circles receives constant press coverage and in the heart of the Vale of Pewsey lies a pub that is very much a part of this unexplained phenomena.

From late spring each year The Barge Inn becomes the centre of attention for thousands of visitors from all over the world who are keen to discover the latest on crop circles, and perhaps witness the most recent of these stunning designs to appear.

Crop circles are by no means a modern phenomenon. About 200 cases were reported prior to 1970 and they are even mentioned in academic texts of the late 17th century. The mystery is who or what created them.

From simple designs such as circles, or circles with rings, they then developed lines. Today they have evolved into breathtaking pictograms with many displaying amazing computer fractals and elements that could only be found in quantum physics processes. The sizes of these stunning creations have also greatly increased with some reported as covering areas of 150,000 - 250,000 sq ft. They generally appear overnight and the sheer complexity of them dismisses the notion that they could possibly be man-made. Hoaxing inevitably occurs frequently but there can be no explanation for the detection of high levels of energy, background radiation, infrared output, and electromagnetism associated with them. It is reported that in 1996 a pilot flew over Stonehenge and saw nothing unusual, but on flying back over the monument 15 minutes later an immense 600 ft series of crop circles had appeared, resembling the Julia Set computer fractal, and comprising of 149 circles.

It is little wonder then that The Barge Inn near Pewsey in Wiltshire has become a mecca for crop circle enthusiasts, being located in a county renowned for numerous sightings. In fact parts of the inn more resemble a research lab than a pub. Giant noticeboards in the pubs 'Crop Room' keep visitors up to date and there are numerous photographs, letters and diagrams everywhere. A huge map covered with coloured stickers details past and present crop circle sightings and the manager has transformed the place into a focal point for the curious hordes who descend on the pub each year.

On the ceiling of the 'Crop Room' is a large impressive mural that depicts the ancient monuments of Wiltshire - Stonehenge, Silbury Hill, Avebury and the White Horse. All are linked together with circles, swirls, and other symbols that have been spotted in local cornfields. The mural was painted by ex-local artist Vince Palmer.

The 'croppies' and professional researchers who visit The Barge Inn are kept well up to date with all local sightings and enthusiasts range from teenagers to the elderly.

Whoever or whatever the reasons behind these beautiful formations, The Barge Inn stands a good chance of being the first to know when that discovery is made.

The isolated Prince of Wales pub and (below) partial views of structures that have long since disappeared into Kenfig Pool and sands.

PRINCE OF WALES
Kenfig, near Porthcawl, South Wales

Originally the medieval town hall and now the only remaining building in a town which has vanished into the sands, the Prince of Wales is part of an enigmatic tale that will both amaze and enchant you.

The pub is located in Kenfig, near Porthcawl which is a popular Welsh seaside resort. Other than a scattering of farmhouses it is all that remains of the ancient city of Kenfig which was swallowed up by the sand dunes running down to the Bristol Channel. Amongst the structures forever lost to the sands was a hospital, church and law courts. The church was built by Morgan Mwyn Mawr who was the founder of Glamorgan as far back as the year 520, and unbelievably Kenfig was once a superb commercial centre of trade. It boasted a river and seaport which were vital for trade links, and an impressive castle that had a gigantic moat.

The first calamity to befall Kenfig arose in 893 when it was almost destroyed by the Vikings. Up to 1402 it is believed to have been razed by fire no less than 8 times, but the greatest damage of all has always been inflicted by the shifting sands. Massive sandstorms were once very frequent and even around 1450 the area was in dire straits with the castle almost overcome by the sands. The immense storm of 1607 finally put paid to what was left of Kenfig and buried almost without trace what little was left of it.

Amazingly the Prince of Wales survived and ever since has been subject to all manner of investigations to ascertain the compounds of its structure - which is believed to contain much of the local once dreaded sand!

The facing picture (bottom) illustrates the expanse of Kenfig Pool with the Bristol Channel further beyond the dunes. The tops of several structures swallowed up are clearly visible and this Atlantis type event has been keenly discussed in local towns for centuries.

The pub has played host to both the local Sunday School and parish council in upstairs rooms and could no doubt tell many a tale of the beleagured Kenfig history.

THE RED LION
Avesbury, Wiltshire

This delightful thatched pub has an unusual claim to fame in that it is set within one of the mysterious circles that comprise the Avesbury Stone Circles. After Stonehenge this is one of Europe's best known archeological features and similarly it is shrouded in mystery as to its exact purpose.

The centuries old history of The Red Lion makes enchanting reading. You can stare into the depths of an historic well in the main bar, or listen to the haunting tales of the 3 resident ghosts - a man, woman and child who are all said to be from the late 1700's.

oldest pubs

THE SKIRRID
Llanvihangel, Crucorney, near Abergavenny, South Wales

The Skirrid is the oldest pub in Wales, has an ancient studded front door, and is located near the base of Skirrid Fawr. It has a long and bloody history as in 1100, a James Crowther was hanged from a beam in the bar for stealing sheep. During the centuries since then over 1,800 more people were hanged in The Skirrid, which was also in use as the local courthouse. All of them met a swift ending by being hanged from the beam above the stairs and the rope mark is clearly visible today as a gruesome reminder. It is thought that the last hanging took place in the late 17th century - also for stealing sheep.

The Inn has also had involvement in the Owain Glyndwr revolt against the rule of Henry IV and the Monmouth Rebellion of the 17th century.

YE OLDE TRIP TO JERUSALEM
1 Brewhouse Yard, Nottingham, Nottinghamshire

This is said by many to be the oldest pub in the country, dating to around 1189. It is a delightful building which has previously done service as a merchant house and watchmaker's. Amongst its other claims to fame are the back rooms that are cut into the sandstone rock below Nottingham Castle, and the unique 'Ring O'Bull' game where you can see how much the ring has eroded the rock. Little nooks and crannies abound here and the history of not only the pub but also the surrounding area can be found in a museum next door. A major tourist attraction and worth seeking out.

THE CLACHAN INN
2 Main Street, Drymen, Glasgow, Scotland

The Clachan Inn is allegedly the oldest in Scotland and was once owned by Rob Roy's sister.

Striking pub sign of The Skirrid and (right) a frontal view of the ancient building.

*Ye Olde Trip To
Jerusalem, England.*

*The Clachan Inn,
Scotland.*

- SPECIAL FEATURE -
THE HISTORY OF PUBS & BEER IN BRITAIN

Beer was brewed by the ancient Egyptians, and it is the consensus of opinion that it had arrived in Britain by the Neolithic period. Over 2,000 years ago when the invading Roman army arrived here they tried to introduce wine by setting up Roman pubs called 'tabernae' (wine shops). The British were not impressed and preferred their beer, but the tabernae eventually gave birth to the idea of the alehouse. At that time beer was brewed everywhere - particularly in farms, and later even by religious bodies such as monasteries.

Various herbs were staple ingredients for flavouring and it was not until the 15th century that hops were imported into England, to be used as both a flavouring and preservative.

As brewing became ever more popular it was inevitable that the dreaded tax collectors would become aware, and as a result their has been a duty levied since 1188 when Henry II introduced the 'Saladin Tithe' to pay for the Crusades.

The magnificent Victorian 'gin palaces' sprang up everywhere with the growth of the railroad, and this is how the large national brewers were able to expand - by following the rail network. There were far too many pubs at that time and they became more and more ornate to attract custom. The splendour of many of these opulent icons of the past can still be seen today but, sadly, they are fast disappearing as major national breweries cater more and more for young clientele.

floor made of gravestones

THE HOP POLE
76 Birmingham Road,
Bromsgrove, Worcestershire

Other than great food The Hop Pole
also has 'Walter the ghost', an original
and quite rare old hop-pole in the
garden, and lastly but certainly not
least the floor of the rear lounge that is
made out of former gravestones.
The reason for this is not known - but
you could always ask!

*Original old hop-pole and (below) a floor
made of former gravestones.*

THE COASTGUARD PUB & RESTAURANT
St.Margaret's Bay, Dover, Kent

This is the closest pub in Britain to France, which is only 20 miles across the English Channel, and it offers absolutely stunning views of both the Straits of Dover and the spectacular chalk cliffs. The area would have been bristling with military activity during both World War's and troop encampments were even stationed nearby during the Napoleonic Wars, such was the strategic importance of this location.

The Coastguard Pub & Restaurant almost certainly has the best outlook of any pub in the country.

THE HOLE IN THE WALL
5 Mepham Street, Waterloo, London SE1

Visitors to this pub will find that it is exactly what its name implies - a hole in the wall. The wall in question is a series of railway arches which are located just outside bustling Waterloo Station, and the pub is actually built into the railway viaduct.

Tired commuters can find solace here in the form of liquid refreshment, although the air is constantly punctuated with the sounds of trains rumbling on the tracks on the bridge overhead - which is the roof of the pub! The Hole in the Wall can be inspirational though if you have yet to book your holidays for the year as the Eurostar makes its way overhead en-route to Paris, whilst you enjoy your drink!

THE GREEN MAN
Harrods Department Store Knightsbridge, London W1

The Green Man is unusual in that it is a pub in a department store, but not any old department store. It is situated in the famous Harrods store in Knightsbridge London, and is a superb period style traditional pub with an eye-catching gilded ceiling and delicately carved wood features.

TIBBIE SHIELS INN
St.Mary's Loch, Selkirkshire, Scotland

A delightful old inn, Tibbie Shiels has been welcoming travellers for over 200 years. It is named in honour of the original owner Isobel (Tibbie) Richardson who moved into what was then known as St.Mary's cottage with her husband Robert, a molecatcher, in 1823. Her husband died suddenly the next year leaving Tibbie with 6 children and almost destitute. She resumed her maiden name, as was the local custom in those days, and set up in business as an innkeeper. Taking in many gentlemen lodgers she catered mainly for the abundance of fishermen who fished the loch, although many of Scotland's most notable literary figures also stayed at the inn.

This small remarkable lady who never re-married died in 1878 aged 96. The inn itself has probably the most striking and unusual location for a pub in Scotland. It is situated overlooking St.Mary's Loch on an isthmus (a narrow strip of land with water both sides) between St.Mary's Loch and Loch of the Lowes, in the Scottish Borders.

what a bore

THE SEVERN BORE INN
Main Road, Minsterworth, Gloucestershire

Most of us will never see a truly huge tidal wave in this country but an equally spectacular and natural event, albeit on a much smaller scale, takes place frequently throughout the year on the River Severn.

A tidal wave known as The Severn Bore makes its way along the river and has been known to reach 2 metres in height. It travels at an average speed of 16 kilometres per hour, and the Severn Estuary is known to have the secong highest tide anywhere in the world. The difference between the highest and lowest tides on any given day can be over 14 metres.

The actual size of the bore can be affected by winds and freshwater levels which can influence both the height and time of the bore. On certain years major bores are anticipated and these draw large crowds of people from all over the country.

Probably the best vantage point of all to witness these exciting events is at The Severn Bore Inn at Minsterworth. It is located right on the banks of the River Severn and has a huge beer garden adjacent to the Severn which provides stunning views.

THE GEORGE INN
4 West Street, Lacock, Wiltshire

The tourist-magnet village of Lacock houses the Fox Talbot Museum of Photography, and also the ancient George Inn which dates from 1361. The centrepiece of this delightful inn is a gigantic fireplace which still boasts a roasting spit and a dog wheel. Extremely rare now, the dog wheel was a horrendous Tudor contraption that any animal lover would despise. It was essentially a small treadmill and is thought to have given rise to the expression - 'its a dogs life'.

The unfortunate canine who had to fit into this tiny thing was a special breed of dog known as a 'turnspit'. They were long-bodied and bandy-legged - no doubt due to the fact that they had to turn the spit that roasted the meat by the fire in unbearable heat. Although this practice was stopped during Victorian times, it was only because of the invention of a mechanical spit.

THE VICTORIA INN
88 Victoria Road, Swindon, Wiltshire

Film buffs who would enjoy a good movie that much more with a pint of real ale in hand should head for The Victoria Inn. The pub has soundproofed its Dungeon Bar and created a cinema that can hold around 35 people. Regular weekly showings that includes the latest releases means visitors can view most films earlier than the satellite channels show them.

The films are shown with a DVD and a £12,000 stereo sound system. It is believed to be the first pub in Britain to be granted special film and music licences which costs The Victoria Inn £700 a year from the Performing Rights Society, the video broadcasting authorities, and Swindon Borough Council. Choc-ices anyone?

canal in a pub

THE CANAL HOUSE
Canal Street, Nottingham, Nottinghamshire

This converted industrial building has a very striking feature - there is actually a canal running through the bar! Visitors will quite often see a boat moored up there as well, so if you are on a boating holiday by canal in Nottingham and want to quench your thirst, why not cruise in!

the spirit of world leaders

THE BERNARD ARMS
**Risborough Road,
Great Kimble, Aylesbury,
Buckinghamshire**

If drinking was once considered a working mans passion then we can now truly abolish that myth with a visit to The Bernard Arms. Photographs on display in the pub show the many notable world leaders to have imbibed here. John Major, Boris Yeltsin, Harold Wilson and Dwight D. Eisenhower to name but a few. It probably helps that the Prime Minister's country residence is only a short way down the road but it still clearly illustrates that a drop of the hard stuff can ensnare even the mighty in its liquid web.

Almost all world leaders who visit Britain want to experience our renowned pubs and sample a pint of bitter or lager. The exception was Boris Yeltsin who preferred vodka. When he visited former Prime Minister John Major they paid a visit to The Bernard Arms. John Major chose a pint but Yeltsin opted for vodka - a bottle of it! The request was initially refused but no doubt for the sake of international relations it was subsequently granted - and Yeltsin got his bottle. For the record the official photograph showed both men with a pint apiece in front of them, as a president who could down a full bottle of vodka in the time it took a prime minister to drink a pint would do little for East-West relations.

Bush, Mitterand and Reagan are other famous leaders to have visited The Bernard Arms, and even George Bush's helicoptor pilot has enjoyed a tipple here. Must be something in the water!

THE BRIDGE INN
**Rose Hill Street, Conwy,
North Wales**

This ever popular pub offers its customers what no other pub in the country can - its very own soap. Not the soap you wash with of course but a Poirot type thing on the internet. As the pub has internet facilities available, customers can catch up with the latest instalments by logging on either here (www.alehouseblues.co.uk) or at home.

Alehouseblues is the usual soap mixture of gossip, sex and scandal, but with an added twist of mystery and intrigue. Past storylines include a barmaid having an affair with a married man - who is playing the Sheriff of Nottingham in the pub panto! The landlord dreams up the plots during lulls in activity at the pub and the site is regularly updated. There are plenty of requests from regulars to be included in the script and many also come up with plot lines and suggestions themselves. They can view the results of these on the computer terminal at the bar. Scripts have even been recorded at the BBC in Bangor, and whilst the viewing figures will never challenge Eastenders or Coronation Street they do at least offer a refreshing change.

THE SHERLOCK HOLMES
10-11 Northumberland Street, Westminster, London WC2

A pub themed on one of the most famous fictional characters in the world has to be a success and in 1957, following its return from a world tour, an entire exhibition that had been assembled for the Festival of Britain was purchased by a brewery whose aim was to create a London theme pub that would attract worldwide Sherlock Holmes enthusiasts.

The inn that had been known as The Northumberland Arms thus became The Sherlock Holmes and with the aid and advice of Sir Arthur Conan Doyle's (Holmes creator) family, the conversion was soon completed.

Adjacent to the restaurant in the pub there is a superb replica of Holmes and Watson's study which is brimming with authentic Victorian artifacts, and the whole place is a shrine to the legend that has arisen around this famous sleuth. Watson's old revolver is on display, as is the stuffed head of the Hound of the Baskervilles - plus an impressive collection of film and television stills and much more.

The reproduction of Holmes study, full of memorabilia.

Old Westons Cider delivery lorry and (below) everything cider related at The Scrumpy House Bar.

cider with rosie

THE SCRUMPY HOUSE BAR
The Bounds, Much Marcle, Ledbury, Herefordshire

This converted 17th century barn is home to a superb cider emporium on the site of a 120 year old family-run cider mill. There is plenty to see here on tours including a working museum and a shop on site that has a plethora of cider related items on sale.

The restaurant offers many speciality dishes - with a few made with Old Rosie Scrumpy.

CIDER CENTRE
Brandy Wharf, Waddingham, Gainsborough, Lincolnshire

One of only a few cider-only pubs in the country, the Cider Centre is a veritable shrine to the drink boasting some 50 dozen or so ciders and perries. All sorts of memorabilia is on show and there is even a small museum. Over 2,000 cider bottles make up a vast collection that has been built up over the years and over 900 of these can be seen displayed. Also look out for the collection of 'Cornish pints' and the foot of 'Cyril the plumber' poking down through the ceiling!

- SPECIAL FEATURE -
THE HISTORY OF CIDER MAKING IN BRITAIN

There is a general consensus of opinion that apple trees grew along the River Nile delta as far back as 1300 BC. Apple growing was originally introduced into Britain by the Druids and different varieties were introduced by the Romans, who after arriving in Britain in 55 BC were said to have found Kentish villagers enjoying a delicious cider-like drink. Julius Caesar is said to have approached the enjoyable pursuit of cider drinking with relish.

At the start of the 9th century cider drinking was very well established in Europe and following the Norman Conquest of 1066, cider consumption was widespread throughout the UK. In fact orchards were established with the sole aim of growing apples for cider production. In medieval times cider making was a thriving industry and monasteries sold immense quantities of it to the public.

The heyday of cider making was probably the mid 17th century when it was even popular to pay part of a farm labourer's wages in cider. Countless farms had their own cider orchard and press and a typical part-wage offering to a farm labourer would be anything between 3-8 pints per day. This practice was abolished in 1887 and profound changes in farming led to a decline in consumption. Cider has now regained its popularity, although sadly it is the mass produced variety that sells most. Traditional cider making is however still flourishing in parts.

It is said that to enjoy a healthy crop of apples the old custom of 'wassailing' (from the Old Englisg 'wes-hal' - be of good health) was practised. Cider soaked pieces of bread were placed in apple tree branches and cider was poured over the roots to encourage good growth. Bonfires were then lit to ward off evil spirits. Even today this tradition still takes place in certain areas.

oldest colony of bees in world

BEEHIVE
Castlegate, Grantham, Lincolnshire

The most remarkable thing about this popular pub is that it has a living pub sign. It is in fact a hive full of bees, mounted in the centre of a lime tree, and resident here since at least 1830 (and probably long before that). This makes it one of the oldest populations of bees in the world. A preservation order was put in place during the 1960's and is believed to be the only one in the country of this nature.

A 'hoody' (beekeeper) tends to the hive and the pub has the history of beehives displayed on its walls.

JEKYLL & HYDE PUB
112 Hanover Street, Edinburgh, Scotland

The Jekyll & Hyde pub is one of many that are in some way connected with, or based on characters created by Scotlands's most famous literary son - Robert Louis Stevenson. Horror movies play constantly at the pub, and the toilets are hidden behind bookcases!

The unforgettable 'Jekyll' and 'Hyde' have long been immortalised in motion pictures. The Strange Case of Dr Jekyll and Mr Hyde was penned by Stevenson following his marriage to Fanny Osborne in 1878, together with other classics such as Treasure Island and Kidnapped. It was Deacon William Brodie (see Deacon Brodies below) who provided the inspiration for Jekyll and Hyde, courtesy of his bizarre double-life.

Born into a famous Edinburgh engineering family, Stevenson was dogged by ill health. He died in Samoa in 1894 but left a legacy of literary genius and was much beloved.

Jekyll & Hyde pub.

DEACON BRODIES
435 Lawnmarket, Edinburgh, Scotland

A cabinet-maker and respected councillor by day, Brodie was a burglar by night. An armed raid on His Majesty's Excise Office proved his downfall and he was hanged in 1788, ironically from a gibbet he had recently redesigned. Robert Louis Stevenson's father had cabinets made by Brodie, and Stevenson used Brodie's split personality as the basis for a book. A huge board outside Deacon Brodies relates his life and subsequent fate.

HAWES INN
Newhalls Road, South Queensferry, near Edinburgh, West Lothian, Scotland

The novel 'Kidnapped' was started here by Stevenson in room 13. The Hawes Inn has one of the most striking locations in the country - in the shadow of the immense Forth road and rail bridges. Nearby boat trips are popular.

a collectors lot

THE YEW TREE INN
Cauldon Waterhouses, Stoke-On-Trent, Staffordshire

One of the most interesting collectors pubs in the country is the The Yew Tree Inn in Cauldon Waterhouses, which appropriately has its namesake right in front of it - a giant Yew Tree. The location alone is unique being situated between an enormous cement works and huge granite quarries, but the interior of the pub simply has to be seen. Such is the sheer oddity of this gem of a pub that it has been featured on Channel 4's Collectors Lot as inside you will find some of the most unusual items to be seen in any pub nationwide.

Working musical instruments (symphonions and polyphons) that are taller than a person, and are certainly something to behold, are merely a few of the many attractions here. Queen Victoria's stockings, pianola's, medieval wind instruments, valuable Staffordshire pottery, old firearms, a boneshaker, longcase clocks, a Jacobean 4-poster bed, an iron dog-carrier, - the list is virtually endless.

Only a visit will enable true appreciation, but be prepared to spend some time here!

Penny Farthing.

Longcase clocks.

Fascinating clutter at The Yew Tree Inn.

get stuffed

JAMAICA INN
Bolventor, Launceston, Cornwall

The Jamaica Inn was built in the mid 18th century on wild and barren Bodmin Moor. Daphne du Maurier, the author of the hugely successful novel 'Jamaica Inn', has a room dedicated to her memory here which has much memorabilia. There is also a highly unusual and delightful attraction called 'Mr Potter's Museum of Curiosity' which is set on 2 floors and has a huge collection of Victorian toys, dolls houses, freaks of nature, smoking memorabilia, strange oddities, etc. The highlight of this impressive collection must be the taxidermy section. Guinea pigs playing cricket and kittens enjoying a cup of tea are just a few of the amazing exhibits on display. The Old School across the road has an impressive theatrical presentation of the Jamaica Inn story presented in tableaux, sound and light, and one of the finest collections of smugglers memorabilia in the country.

THE DROVERS INN
Inverarnan, Loch Lomond, Scotland

Visitors are sure to have the feeling that externally, The Drovers Arms has remained untouched for decades, and this feeling will certainly prevail when entering the pub. You are greeted at the entrance hall by the outstretched arms of a stuffed grizzly bear standing on its hind legs, whilst multiple stuffed birds and small animals stare at you with beady eyes from glass fronted display cabinets. The overall impression is one of timelessness and the bar area is little different. Apart from welcoming fires it has a stuffed golden eagle to admire perched at the end of it. All of this is greatly enhanced by staff in traditional kilts and sometimes piped Scottish music that welcomes all visitors, including many climbers and walkers.

HIGHWAYMAN
Sourton, Devon

The Highwayman is one of those curiosity pubs that ensures several visits are required to truly satisfy inquisitive minds. The pub has a remarkable design that has been constantly bettered by over 40 years of input from the owners. The interior is a warren of flagstone floored intimate rooms with stuffed animals, intricately carved pews and other delightfully varied seating, plus quaint bow windows amongst much more that there is to admire. Also look out for 'Rita Jones Locker' which is an imitation sailing galleon that must be seen.

ELEPHANTS NEST
Horndon, Marytavy, Tavistock, Devon

This unspoilt 400 year old pub has its name written on the beams in about 60 different languages, all done by a succession of different visitors - and even some by old landlords.

headline news

THE STAR INN
Manor Road, Sulgrave,
near Banbury,
Northamptonshire

There are plenty of curios and oddities in this former farmhouse to keep your attention for a week. The most bizarre must be the many newspaper front pages on display that have headlines screaming out such things as the first hole in the heart operation, Kennedy's assassination, and the death of Churchill.

Weird stuffed animals include a hare's head with small antlers fitted to make it resemble a tiny stag, the backside of a fox appearing to jump through the wall, and a kangaroo with a hanging-corks hat. They certainly make you stop and think. A blackboard usually displays a weird and obscure fact of the day.

Old newspaper headlines and a collection of the bizarre at The Star Inn including (below) an old gas mask and helmet.

strangest pub sign

The Chequered Skipper. Not a pub to get 'hammered' in!

THE CHEQUERED SKIPPER
The Green, Ashton Oundle, Peterborough, Cambridgeshire

This is probably the most unique pub sign in the country. Full size, it depicts a colourful butterfly and is made completely out of many different types of nails.

FOX & HOUNDS
High Street, Barley, Royston, Hertfordshire

The Fox & Hounds at Barley has a famous and very rare gallows pub sign which is a beam that traverses the road. The carvings are superb in a depiction of a hunting scene that has a fox being chased by 2 huntsmen on horseback and a pack of dogs.

The origins of pub and inn signs can be traced back to the Romans when vine leaves were displayed to indicate that they sold wine. Subsequently in Britain small evergreen bushes were used.

As the naming of inns and alehouses became popular by the 12th century, signs were also added. This was common practice as most of the population could neither read or write. In 1393 an Act was passed making it compulsory for a sign to be displayed for identification purposes.

Before the Reformation many inn signs followed a religious theme, but when Henry split with the Catholic church numerous King's Heads and Crown's became popular as signs.

The Victorian era saw much competition for trade as countless 'gin palaces' sprang up. As interiors became more extravagant the inn signs followed suit. Signs got so large and imposing that eventually there were ordinances against them as they were considered dangerous. Very few of these colossal gallows signs exist today.

grotesque gargoyles

NUT TREE
Murcott, near Kidlington, Oxfordshire

The Nut Tree has a striking collection of unusual gargoyles which were once hung from a walnut tree, but now lie scattered in the undergrowth ready to startle unsuspecting passers by. They are each modelled on actual local characters, although it is doubtful if anyone is likely to admit one of these grotesque creations is in their image.

The gargoyles were carved by a Canadian sculptor named Frederick Close who stayed in the area some years ago. Magnificently carved, they certainly provide a talking point for new visitors.

mind the doors

PRINCE ALFRED
5a Formosa Street,
Maida Vale, London W9

Little altered since it was built in 1863 this classic Victorian pub is sure to delight traditionalists. There are 5 bars, each unusually with their own street entrance. To move from bar to bar internally you have to stoop through tiny, roughly waist-height doors in the partitions. Intended for access for the cleaners, they clearly illustrate the divisions that were apparent in Victorian society of bygone days. The original Private bar can be seen and even the Ladies bar complete with 'snob-screens', which were the order of the day to ensure a discreet level of privacy.

There are impressive reminders of Victorian pub heritage and drinking culture everywhere. Carved fixtures and fittings, exquisitely etched glass, even the external standard lamps. A marvel of period design, the entire weight of all the upper floors is supported by lintels on thin iron columns.

The pub was actually named after Queen Victoria's second son who became Duke of Edinburgh in 1862 at the tender age of 18.

THE BELL
The Street,
Waltham St.Lawrence,
Reading, Berkshire

The partly timbered Bell Inn was donated to the village by Ralph Newbery in 1633 and is one of the finest preserved examples of a Tudor interior of any building in England today. History abounds here - even the adjacent church was mentioned in the Domesday Book. The pub was originally constructed in 1380 and features a delightful, rare curved door that leads into the main rooms. Evidence of the legacy left in trust to the village is the original charter that can be seen in the pub. It indicates that it was set up to support charities, and the rent has been donated thus ever since.

The Bell is one of those historic English treasures that every person should see at least once in their lifetime.

WHITE HART INN
Nant-y-Ceisaid, Machen,
South Wales

A plethora of ship's memorabilia greets visitors to the White Hart Inn which adds to the genuine feel of being on a liner! In fact the panelling that can be seen throughout was salvaged from an ocean going liner that was dismantled at nearby Newport Docks. The 'sea-legs' feeling will grow on you as you walk down the long narrow corridor and discover the hugely impressive bar - which will rekindle thoughts of the Titanic film of not so long ago, for those of you who have seen it.

A very pleasant unassuming pub found between Caerphilly and Newport, this is sure to appeal to sea-dogs everywhere.

massive water wheels

EGYPT MILL
Stroud Road, Nailsworth, Gloucestershire

It has been suggested that early Egyptian travellers settled on the river banks, thus giving the area - and subsequently the mill - its name. However, just how the property became known as 'Egypt' still remains a mystery. Back in 1675 the building then contained 2 fulling mills, a gig mill and a dyehouse. Today, gigantic working waterwheels with the millstream flowing through are very impressive sights at this converted stone structured mill. Old ironwork from the mill machinery and split level views of the waterwheels in motion are well worth seeing.

MOOR MILL
Smugoak Lane, Bricket Wood, St.Albans, Hertfordshire

This converted 18th century mill dates from about 1762, although a mill is believed to have stood on this site for over 1,000 years. Apart from the many original features that remain, visitors here can also see a huge working mill wheel ploughing through the water from a glassed vantage point in the pub.

Giant water wheels provide a topic for conversation at the Egypt Mill.

grate place to hide

THE LORD CREWE ARMS HOTEL
Blanchland, near Consett, Durham

The gigantic fireplace at The Lord Crewe Arms Hotel is believed to be the largest in the country and conceals a 'Priesthole' where Tom Forster, the leader of the local Jacobites, evaded capture by the King's forces during the uprising of 1715, although he later surrendered and was imprisoned. Once part of a 13th century monastery The Lord Crewe Arms Hotel has many unusual features including a huge barrel vaulted crypt bar.

Blanchland, named for the 'white monks' who occupied the ruined abbey at its centre, is full of history which includes the pillaging by Scots in 1296. The gardens behind The Lord Crewe Arms Hotel were once the cloisters of the abbey, treaded in solitude by the monks of Blanchland.

A most traditional inn, amongst other attractions is the resident ghost of a woman - not just any woman but Dorothy Forster, Lord Crewe's wife and the sister of Tom Forster. She rode to London in disguise as a servant, obtained duplicate keys, and aided her brother to escape prison and flee to France for his safety. She is now said to haunt the Bamburgh Room of The Lord Crewe Arms Hotel awaiting news of her brother.

london calling

CROCKER'S FOLLY
**24 Aberdeen Place,
London NW8**

Frank Crocker was a man with an eye for an opportunity and when he found out that the new railway terminus was to be built opposite, he knew his hotel would be a roaring success. The opulent Crown Hotel was subsequently buit in a riot of Victorian splendour and with no expense spared. Over 50 types of marble were used and almost every part of the structure was encased in marble - columns, the bar counter, chimney-piece, even the walls. Added to this was an extravaganza of highly ornate plaster mouldings and reliefs, the finest quality woods including delicately carved mahogany, and an entrance hall befitting kings and queens.

Tragically, the railway terminus was constructed over half a mile away at Marylebone, and Crocker, in total despair and by now almost penniless, hurled himself from an upstairs window.

The name of the pub now is indicative of man's folly in the single-minded pursuit of a goal. It is also however a splendid legacy for other generations to enjoy.

THE BLACK FRIAR
**174 Queen Victoria Street,
London EC4**

Built around 1875 on the old site of 13th century Dominican Priory this 'cheese-wedge' shaped pub is extravagance at its finest. The numerous illustrations and carvings of merry monks, which reflect its origins, were the inspirational work of Royal Academy sculptor Henry Poole.

Almost all the carvings date from 1905 and the pub is truly an art-nouveau masterpiece. There are monks at play, monks harvesting, monks singing carols - even the light fittings are carved monks and the detail is simply amazing. The stunning mosaic ceiling is another superb attraction.

VIADUCT TAVERN
**126 Newgate Street,
London EC1**

The Holborn Viaduct opened by the Queen in 1869 led to the naming of this pub. The carvings and gilding here are delightful and many original features still survive today including paintings of maidens depicting agriculture, the arts and banking.

Both the Viaduct Tavern and the famous Old Bailey (opposite) were constructed on the site of the notorious Newgate Prison where conditions were horrendous and hangings continued until 1868. Visitors to the Viaduct Tavern can even have a tour of the former prison cells which are located in what is now the cellars of the pub.

LAMB
**94 Lamb's Conduit Street,
London WC1**

A visit to the Lamb is as near as is possible to a return to Victorian times. The pub and street it is located on are named after William Lamb who brought fresh water to the district of Holborn back in 1577. The pub is most famous for what are probably the finest examples of swivelling cut glass 'snob-screens' in the country. They run the whole length of the bar counter.

deepest well

MILBURY'S
Beauworth, near Sheriton, Hampshire

A Bronze Age cemetery surrounds this pub which achieved a degree of fame in 1833 when a hoard of 6,000 silver coins was found there. On a more up to date note this popular pub has a 300 year old well (with a massive treadmill) which is 302ft deep. It is said that if you drop a coin into the spotlit shaft it would take about 8-10 seconds to reach the bottom, depending on the height of the fast flowing stream below!

Enormous treadmill and (below) a barely visible shaft of light at the bottom of the 302ft well at Milbury's.

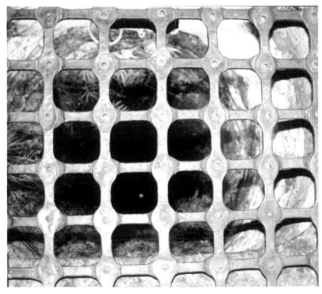

egypt & the nile

THE NILE
9-21 Castle Street, Inverness, Highlands, Scotland

For a taste of Egypt visit the Scottish Highlands! This is not as crazy as it sounds as The Nile bar in Inverness is a superb Egyptian orientated experience where visitors can see an entire bar front resembling carved out sandstone blocks, a sarcophagus, and numerous hieroglyphics. The pictures on the walls of old Egyptians remind you of a Cairo bazaar and there is certainly no other place quite like this.

The phrase 'walk like an Egyptian' could well have originated here after one too many!

THE BAG O'NAILS
141 St. Georges Street, Hotwells, Bristol

Previously known as The American Eagle this traditional single room pub is one of very few to still retain old gas lighting. It was a previous regional Camra Pub of the Year winner, which must mean the ales are pretty good, and the cellar dispensing these ales can be viewed from various vantage points in the bar by peering down through port-holes in the bare wooden flooring.

THE WHITE SWAN
34 Frenchgate, Doncaster, Yorkshire

The small front room type bar at the White Swan has, reputedly, the tallest bar in Britain at about 5ft in height. Stiletto shoes help here then!

OLDE FERRY BOAT INN
Holywell, near St.Ives, Cambridgeshire

This is one of the oldest inns in the country, with some people even saying it is the oldest. It can be dated back to at least 1068 with a disputed history that stretches back in time to the 6th century. The inn is reputedly haunted - particularly on the 17th March - by the ghost of Juliet Tewsley, a yound lady who hung herself from a nearby tree on that date in 1050 when her attentions were rejected by a local woodcutter. The Olde Ferry Boat Inn is built over her grave and a slab in the centre of the main bar marks her burial spot.

This ancient building has everything you would associate with such a great age and is well worth a visit - but not on 17th March!

THE KING STREET RUN
86 King Street, Cambridge, Cambridgeshire

Once called the Horse and Groom, this pub is now renowned for the heights of eccentricity that it scales. The extremely odd interior has upside down shelves, reverse signs on the toilet doors (where you could be some time 'pulling' instead of 'pushing'), and holes in the downstairs ceiling which provide views of the equally bizarre upstairs bar. In fact upstairs is somewhat modelled on a junk-yard, complete with a fake corrugated roof!

The King Street Run is truly a pub that has to be seen to be believed.

MORRITT ARMS
Greta Bridge, Durham

The Morritt Arms is an old coaching inn which is named in honour of Charles Dickens who stayed here in 1838 whilst on his way to start researching for his book, Nicholas Nickleby.

All around the walls is a spectacular lengthy Dickensian mural painted in 1946 by J.V.Gilroy, who incidentally also has six of his old Guinness adverts on display here which he was more famous for.

GEORGE HOTEL
Land Of Green Ginger, Hull, Humberside

Dating back to 1683 this former Elizabethan mansion has 4 intriguing mysteries that visitors may care to solve - as well as what is probably the smallest window in England that measures just half an inch wide by 13 inches in length. It may have been a look in/out port when the George was a coach house.

Dramatic Dickensian mural.

pub in a museum

NEW INN
Blists Hill Open Air Museum, Ironbridge, Telford, Shropshire

The New Inn is actually a reconstructed 19th century public house from Green Lane, Walsall and was opened for business at Blists Hill Open Air Museum in March 1983. A number of potential pubs were considered before this was selected and moved brick by brick (as with many of the other buildings here) to its present location.

The scrubbed wood and sawdust covered floors appear very much as they would have done many years ago, and a pewter measure of 'mother's ruin' can be bought for about 3d (3 pence in old money prior to decimilisation). You can change sterling into this old currency at the local bank on site and it can be spent at the bakery, chemist, and a host of other attractions.

Staff at the pub wear authentic period dress and it is startling to see this former predominantly male preserve, with many original parts, as it would have appeared in the intervening years since its original construction about 1880.

THE BRAM STOKER TAVERN
148 Old Brompton Road, Kensington, London SW5

Gothic does not come any better than this. The Dracula theme at The Bram Stoker Tavern is fascinating, eerie, and most compelling with a waxwork model of the master himself looking down over a scene that includes a reproduction of a private library, scientific odds and ends, and much creepy memorabilia - all in an impressive setting. Silent horror classics can be seen constantly on the television, and even the outward appearance of the building itself plays a major part in the realistic 'fangs and fiends' atmosphere. Must be seen.

eerie medieval crypt

WATERGATES WINE BAR
11-13 Watergate Street, Chester, Cheshire

This bar and restaurant is set within what is said to be the oldest medieval crypt in England. Gothic archways, three long tunnels, and eerie lighting create a haunting, gloomy atmosphere in this building that dates back to 1120.

It was in use as a morgue in the 1960's and there is said to be a ghost here. What is known is that a dead body was found under one of the floor flagstones in the 1800's, and it was then replaced and the flagstone dated!

ploughing the waves

THE PILCHARD INN
Burgh Island, Bigbury on Sea, Devon

This famous 14th century white walled pub is located on a small tidal island and can can only be reached, when the tide is in, by enjoying a ride on a giant sea-tractor. At other times visitors can walk across the sandy causeway.

Pirates and smugglers once used the island as a base as the tides and currents made it secure, and the famous writer Agatha Christie was a regular visitor here. Burgh Island lies several hundred yards off the coast at Bigbury on Sea and was even commandeered by the Army during the Second World War due to its strategic importance.

bath time at horse & jockey

HORSE & JOCKEY
Woodstock Road, Oxford, Oxfordshire

This extremely eccentric pub has a motley assortment of bizarre furnishings and decor. In fact decor, if that is an adequate word to decribe what you see at the Horse & Jockey, consists of most of the walls and ceilings covered with newspapers and bare light fittings. A bath on its end, outsize games, and a few more surprises are in store here.

monkeying about

MONKEY HOUSE
Defford, Worcestershire

This is one of very few remaining, absolutely traditional cider houses and its name is taken from a story that tells of a drunken customer who fell into some bramble bushes many years ago - and swore he was attacked by monkeys! At the end of a group of cottages, the pub has been in the same family for over 140 years and the only clue that it is in fact a pub from the outside is the 'Licensed to sell cider and tobacco' sign above the door.

Cider is tapped by barrels and poured into pottery mugs, and the endearing charm of the Monkey House is sure to appeal to all traditionalists.

THE BALTIC FLEET
Wapping, Liverpool, Merseyside

This imposing Victorian tavern was built in the late 1840's and is a unique Grade II Listed sandstone building that has been a waterfront landmark in Liverpool for generations. It is said to have more entrances (7 at the last count) than any other pub in Liverpool, and the old school furniture which includes tables, chairs and benches provided for patrons use, is quite novel. It has extensive tunnels out of the cellars which probably have smuggling connections, and was named after the Baltic Fleet - a huge combined Fleet which sailed to the Baltic during the Crimean War under the command of Admiral Sir Charles Napier, who was born in Liverpool.

THE WHITE BULL
Ribchester, Lancashire

A stuffed fox in 2 halves that appears to be jumping through the wall is a novelty that should raise a smile at the White Bull in Ribchester. The attractions of this superb 18th century establishment are many and being situated in a former Roman town there is certainly an abundance of history here. The Tuscan entrance pillars have stood here for about 2,000 years and visitors may also like to see the remains of a Roman bath house, plus a Roman museum nearby.

THE FOUR MARYS
65 High Street, Linlithgow, Scotland

A very atmospheric pub, this is named after the 4 ladies-in-waiting to Mary Queen of Scots who was born in nearby Linlithgow Palace.

Apart from many superb antiques and some remarkable masonry, the pub has masses of memorabilia relating to the doomed queen such as a facsimile of her death-mask and a piece of bed curtain amongst others.

THREE ELMS
North Wootton, Sherborne, Dorset

A highly impressive collection of model cars and other vehicles are on show here, and the gent's and ladies toilets have a saucy collection of over 500 seaside postcards to admire - whilst you go about your business!

world's first robotic bar

CYNTHIA'S BAR & RESTAURANT
4 Tooley Street, London SE1

Located on Tooley Street in the vaults below London Bridge (which is also home to the well known 'London Dungeon') is Cynthia's Bar & Restaurant - the world's first robotic bar! Actually there are 2 robot operated bars here called Cynthia's and Rastus, in addition to the Star Lounge (shaped like a star) and an impressive restaurant.

Your whizzing and whirring metallic bar person says hello and actually talks to you whilst your cocktail is being mixed in under 60 seconds!

THE SPANISH GALLEON
48 Greenwich Church Street, Greenwich, London SE10

A splendid old tavern, The Spanish Galleon can be dated back to about 1834 although a 'Spanish Galleon' is believed to have been in existence nearby at least 150 years before that. Following some work that was being done in the cellars a bricked up room was discovered, and inside in excellent condition was a preserved sailor's uniform dating from about 1850. This can now be viewed in the bar.
Also discovered was a secret tunnel that is believed to lead to the Royal Naval College which is only a short way down the road.

THE WHITE HART
Worthgate Place, Canterbury, Kent

Reputedly haunted, The White Hart is built on the ruins of St.Mary's Church and is located only about a mile from Canterbury Cathedral. The cellar here was once the mortuary to the church and it still has the body chute in place! The small adjacent park was the graveyard where tombstones can still be seen along the wall. On the other side is an ancient Roman burial site.

PACK HORSE
South Stoke, Somerset

This welcoming, over 500 years old pub, was originally constructed by the priory to provide respite for travellers.
The entrance alleyway that runs through the centre of the Pack Horse is still a public right of way to the church, and it is also where the dead used to be carried along to the cemetery. Ancient features abound in this pub and the cupboard by the fireplace is said to have been where drunks were kept until they sobered up!

THE HINDS HEAD
Wasing Lane, Aldermaston, Berkshire

The cave looking dining area at The Hinds Head is the former village lock-up which was last in use, as such, circa 1865. This 16th century inn also features a clock and belltower.

antique musical museum

THE CROOK INN
Tweedsmuir,
near Moffat, Borders,
Scotland

The Crook Inn vies with The Clachan Inn (page 52) for the claim of being Scotland's oldest licenced inn. Refurbished in art deco style in 1936, the pub is a splendid example of period grandeur with magnificent etched mirrors and superb fittings throughout. The ladies and gents toilets are fine examples of this!

The inn is 17th and 18th century in parts and is famous for its River Tweed setting. It is known that Robert Burns wrote his famous 'Willie Wastles Wife' poem here.

THE GEORGE
St.Briavels, Gloucestershire

The George overlooks 12th century St.Briavels Castle and has much to admire. When a fireplace was removed a Celtic coffin lid was discovered and it is believed to date from 1070. It is now on display set into a wall in the bar.

THREE HORSESHOES
Bridge Street,
Warham Village, Norfolk

Automic organs, pianos, musical boxes and much more can be seen at the wind-up gramaphone museum at the Three Horseshoes. There are even antique one-arm bandits in the pub itself.

Wind-up gramaphone museum at the Three Horseshoes.

patriotic

THE UNION INN
Tamar Street, Waterside, Saltash, Cornwall

The Union Inn can be found on the historic Waterside at Saltash, impressively positioned to the western side of the River Tamar which forms the boundary line between Devon and Cornwall. It lies in the shadows of 2 gigantic bridges; the Tamar Suspension Bridge opened in 1961 to meet the growing demand of motorists, and the Prince Albert Railway Bridge designed by Isambard Kingdom Brunel and opened in 1859.

Equally as dominating a sight as the bridge's, The Union Inn has a striking Union Jack painted and emblazoned over the whole of the front of the pub. It is recorded as having been painted in 1995 to mark the 50th anniversary of V.E.Day, and not for attention-seeking reasons - although it no doubt draws many a backward glance from those crossing the river by car or rail.

The entire east wall of the pub is taken up with a gigantic mural instigated by former Saltash Mayor Peter Stephens, and painted by local artist David Whitley over the course of 3 months. It depicts Saltash through the ages and includes old customers alongside more famous faces such as Sir Francis Drake and Isambard Kingdom Brunel.

Pictures inside The Union Inn depict the colourful history of the Waterside and how times have changed since the turn of the century. Roundheads and Cavaliers previously fought over Saltash in a series of bloody encounters with one battle alone reputed to have claimed over 700 lives, right here at the Waterside.

Although some may describe it as mildly eccentric, the pub is a hive of activity and does much to support local good causes.

The Union Inn - an unmistakable landmark.

celebrity footwear

THE BOOT INN
Barnard Gate, Witney, Oxfordshire

There is a highly unusual and fascinating collection of footwear that has been donated by dozens of famous people including many pop stars, sportsmen and women, plus TV personalities at the appropriately named Boot Inn.

Stars such as the Bee Gees, Jeremy Clarkson, George Best, Ronnie Barker, Clive James and Geoff Hurst are amongst the many other celebrities whose choice of footwear is made public here. All labelled and well displayed, they are certain to provide a main talking point for any visitors.

ALLENHEADS INN
Allenheads, Hexham, Northumberland

This amazing pub, courtesy of the renowned 'nutty' landlord, has every available space on the walls, ceilings, and it seems everywhere else covered with more than 5,000 collectibles ranging from a 4ft wooden chicken to long silenced musical instruments. There is no specific order here and visitors will find antique furniture in the dining room together with a plastic snake! It is truly an Alladin's cave of memorabilia where the probability is that any item that comes into your head stands a good chance of being on display. Typewriters, stuffed animals, old radios, mangles, a ship's wheel, birdcages, shoes, an engine-room telegraph - even a vintage Rolls Royce parked outside. The list is endless and the pub has to be seen.

CROWS NEST
Crows Nest, Darite, Cornwall

This quaintly old fashioned pub was formerly the pay office and company store where local tin miners were paid. Apart from the obvious memorabilia connected with the tin mining industry there is also a highly unusual table which was converted from a huge blacksmith's bellows. Incidentally the bellows still work.

BULL i'TH' THORN
Buxton, Derbyshire

Apart from its name there is a lot more of the bizarre to be found at the Bull i'th' Thorn. There are highly unusual carvings at the main entrance including one of a bull caught in a thornbush, another of some dogs chasing a rabbit, and an eagle with a freshly caught hare. The huge hall which dates from 1471 has a gigantic central beam which runs parallel with many smaller ones, and there are many impressive features to admire such as the ornately carved hunting chair, panelled window seats, and a huge open fire. Much armour, 17th century German helmets, and even blunderbusses are on display.

PLOUGH
Great Munden, near Ware, Hertfordshire

The largest musical 'instrument' in any pub in the country is the unique full size working Compton theatre organ that can be seen (and frequently heard) in the specially built extension at the Plough.

CAFE ROYAL
West Register Street,
Edinburgh, Scotland

One of the most opulent Victorian bars in Scotland, the Cafe Royal has a superb and enormous period island bar in addition to many attractive and original fittings. Its most prominent features are the large tiled murals with hand painted Doulton Faience tiles.

The murals, by John Eyre, portray William Caxton, Benjamin Franklin, Robert Peel, Michael Faraday, George Stephenson and James Watt.
All famous inventors, they are each depicted at their moment of discovery.

*Superb and rare
Doulton Faience tiled
murals by John Eyre.*

bear pit

THE WHITE HART
**82 Market Street,
Ashby De La Zouch,
Leicestershire**

Once Dick Turpin's favourite drinking house, The White Hart has an old historic artesian well and a partly covered old bear pit. An enormous stuffed bear depicts what the scene may have looked like many years ago.

KINGS ARMS
**Westgate Street, Blakeney,
Norfolk**

Apart from the theatrical memorabilia that is on show the Kings Arms lays claim to fame for having the smallest art gallery in the country - housed in a former telephone kiosk!

COBWEB INN
**Penhally Hill, Boscastle,
Cornwall**

This former warehouse is one of the most colourful and interesting pubs in Cornwall and at one time it had real cobwebs throughout the building that were occupied by massive spiders. It is said that neither the staff or customers were permitted to destroy a cobweb or there would be big trouble.

The pub is of course much more pleasant nowadays and some of its current unusual features are the large collection of hundreds of colourful old bottles hanging from the beams in the bar, and an enormous armchair that has been completely carved out of a tree-trunk.

EIGHT BELLS
**Church Street,
Chipping Campden,
Gloucestershire**

Of the 3 stone fireplaces at the Eight Bells, the gigantic one has a painting of the pub in summer. The heavy old oak beams with enormous timber supports indicate a great age, and this is verified by the glass covered section of floor that shows part of the secret passage which Roman Catholic Priests used to escape from the Roundheads.

BULLS HEAD
**Harborough Road, Clipston,
Market Harborough,
Leicestershire**

A strange tradition was started by US airmen who were based in the vicinity during World War II when they used to wedge coins in the spaces of the old woodwork here. Hundreds of coins now glint from the dark beams of this welcoming village inn.

THE PILLARS
**9 & 15 Crichton Street,
Dundee, Scotland**

This late 18th century building has a model of the Old Town House (known affectionately as the 'Pillars') located over the main entrance door.

Unusual is the fact that the bar entrance is at 9 Crichton Street with the lounge entrance located at 15 Crichton Street. They are connected by the upper lounge to the rear of the building - with a Driving School below them in the middle!

Old bear pit at The White Hart.

Smallest art gallery in the country?

Secret underground passage at the Eight Bells.

seconds out at royal oak

ROYAL OAK
200 The Broadway, Cardiff, South Wales

Hardly altered since well before the turn of the century this remarkable pub even has its own professional boxing gym. The pub itself is a sporting shrine, with boxing in particular taking pride of place. Pictures of famous boxers from all over the world jostle with a magnificent range of memorabilia for wall space and there is hardly a square inch of flock wallpaper to be seen.

'Peerless' Jim Driscoll's career is recorded on the walls of the bar and he was once himself a Cardiff licensee. He is immortalised with a lifesize statue just outside The Golden Cross public house (also on this page) which stands at the gateway to the impressive Cardiff Bay Development.

Worth noting at the Royal Oak are the intricate stained glass screens behind the bar which have shielded the windows for over a hundred years.

GOLDEN CROSS
283 Hayes Bridge Road, Cardiff, South Wales

A Listed building that boasts a huge Victorian tiled picture of Cardiff Castle, the old Golden Cross pub is a splendid icon of a truly unspoilt traditional drinking establishment and has overcome many a determined planning application. Impressive architectural features abound here and the whole ground floor Doulton Faience exterior and interior is completely covered in one of the finest and most complete examples of period tiling in the country. An ideal pub for a night on the tiles!

husky dogs

THE SPORTSMAN'S ARMS
Bylchau, Denbigh Moors, Conwy, North Wales

The Sportsman's Arms is the highest pub in Wales and during summer people visit here from all over the world. Remarkably, during winter, husky dog teams compete in dog-sled trials. The ever popular RAC Rally is also right on the pubs doorstep.

THE DOVECOTE
Laxton, Nottinghamshire

The village of Laxton hosts a very odd annual event! A visitor centre behind The Dovecote will relate that Laxton is the only place in the country that still operates the ancient open field farming system, part of which entails that the grass is auctioned off for haymaking during late June each year. As a result of this anyone who lives in the local parish would be entitled to not only a bid, but also a free drink at the pub! During this time a court is held at the pub with a Clerk of the Court sitting to settle any disputes between farmers, etc. Fines of a few pence are often imposed!

The pub and surrounding villages are all Crown property and hence are effectively owned by the Queen. Laxton is also one of the highest points in Nottinghamshire and the views are quite stunning.

THE FAT LAMB
Crossbank, Ravenstonedale, Kirkby Stephen, Cumbria

This traditional country inn is set in superb surroundings between the Lake District and Yorkshire Dales. It must be the only pub in the country that has a private 15 acre nature reserve that visitors can ramble through and enjoy.

THE RAILWAY INN
High Street, Llangefni, Anglesey, North Wales

Situated on a hill near an important market town is The Railway Inn. It is actually built into the hillside with the exposed rock being the bar wall.

THE OLDE SHIP
7 Main Street, Seahouses, Northumberland

Built in 1745, visitors to The Olde Ship will discover a veritable feast of nautical memorabilia. The items have been collected over a number of years and include ship's wheels, figureheads, lifeboat oars, etc. There is even a museum upstairs with yet more artifacts. The pub has been in the same family since 1910.

Lindisfarne (Holy Island) can be visited via a causeway when the tide is out. It boasts the largest flock of wintering geese in Britain in addition to cormorants, whooper swans and other breeds. It is also possible to get a boat to Farne Islands which also has numerous colonies of birds, as well as endearing seals.

grave-robbing

BEN CROUCH TAVERN
77a Wells Street, London W1

The grave-robbing themed bar that is The Ben Crouch Tavern is actually based on a real character. Ben Crouch promoted boxing at the turn of the 1800's but was known as the 'king of the reserrectionists', probably because he had the monopoly on supplying cadavers to local hospitals for research and experiments.

There are quite a few large gargoyles and shock-horror memorabilia scattered around the pub in addition to a gruesome depiction of Ben Crouch himself. This is also the meeting place of the London Vampyre Group who congregate here on the second Thursday of every month.

take a seat

THE CRAB & LOBSTER
**Disforth Road, Asenby,
near Thirsk, Yorkshire**

The Crab & Lobster has an abundance of odd curiosities on display. There is also an interesting array of seating that includes settees, antique high-backed chairs, theatrical corner seats and even a dentist's chair!

WEST ARMS
**Llanarmon Dyffryn Ceiriog,
Llangollen, North Wales**

Dating back to the 16th century, the West Arms is full of antique settle seating and has an enormous elaborately carved confessional stall in the bar, possibly of Catholic origin.

*Huge confessional stall
at the West Arms.*

RED LION HOTEL
**1 Old Hall Street,
Malpas, Cheshire**

The chair King James I used is still here and a tradition states that if you sit in the chair you must pay a penny for the privilege - or pay for a round of drinks for everyone!

BLACK HORSE
**Clevedon Lane,
Clapton-in-Gordano,
near Bristol**

A snug at the Black Horse has a window that is barred from when it was formerly the local petty-sessions gaol, and a settle in this room boasts a stunning carved creature.

EAGLE & CHILD INN
**1 Church Road, Wharles,
Preston, Lancashire**

A settle at the Eagle & Child Inn came from a stately home in Staffordshire. The head of the family who owned it had an argument with his cook, killed him, and because of this the King ordered that the family change their coat-of-arms by adding a shield depicting a bloody hand. It is said that this man was the Governor of Ireland at the time, and that red hand is depicted on the Ulster flag today. The coat-of-arms can be seen on the settle in the pub together with the red hand.

liars & charmers

THE BRIDGE INN
Santon Bridge, Holmrook, Wasdale, Cumbria

During mid November each year when the Western Lakes and Fells can be at their spectacular best, The Bridge Inn at Santon Bridge plays host to the most peculiar of all competitions - 'The World's Biggest Liar'.

Back in the 19th century a well known Cumbrian named Will Ritson (1808-1890) was a popular publican at the head of the Wasdale Valley. His customers were always kept amused with delightful stories of the folk heritage of the area, and being a sincere and honest man who always insisted his tales were true, listeners had no reason to doubt him. One of Will's claims was that the turnips in Wasdale were so big they could be used as sheds for the sheep from the fells.

In honour of 'Auld Will' and his fabulous yarns, the annual competition of 'The World's Biggest Liar' is held at The Bridge Inn, and people do indeed visit from all over the world to hear enlightened facts such as how the Lake District was formed - not by ice or volcanic activity, but by large moles and eels!

The current landlord here is said to be 192 years old, and strange crossbreeds of rabbits and alsations work as sheep dogs on the fells!

THE NORMANDY ARMS
Chapel Street, Blackawton, Totnes, Devon

May Bank Holiday (the first Monday in the month of May) is the time of year when visitors and those just passing through the village of Blackawton will witness a quite bizarre spectacle. Now in its second decade, the Blackawton International Festival of Wormcharming is an event that will strike horror into the hearts of those with an aversion to all things 'creepy-crawlie'. Not to be confused with similar events held 'up North' where the rules are quite different, the festival at The Normandy Arms is British eccentricity at its finest.

Teams consist of a 'Charmer', 'Catcher' and a 'Counter'. The area that is to be charmed by each team is a maximum of 3ft x 4ft and is referred to as 'The Plot'. The alloted time is 15 minutes per team and the Charmer uses a solution to dampen the soil. Another act called 'twanging' involves hand vibrating a garden fork into the turf.

The British Association of Worm Length Supporters (BAWLS) decree that all worms have to be returned to the ground at the end of the contest when the team having charmed the greatest number of worms in the alloted time is the winner. It is on record that in 1980, at another competition, someone once charmed 511 worms from their slumber to see what all the commotion was about!

BAROQUE
34 Low Row, Sunderland, Tyne & Wear

When renovations were commenced at the old church hall that is now Baroque, 2 long corridors were discovered underground with a series of crypts leading off, with the bodies still in them! This gothic theme has been adopted by Baroque - specially commissioned gargoyles with fibre optic eyes are just one of the many stunning features to be found here.

The most unusual places to visit below ground - and all open to the public including: a complete street of shops and houses sealed and entombed following the plague. Massive power stations in hollow mountains. Secret nucluer command centres. Neanderthal caves, secret passages, and even a Viking settlement. Objects turning to stone before your very eyes. Dungeons . . . .

STRANGEST
UNDERGROUND PLACES IN BRITAIN
– seeing is believing –

. . . prisons and amazing phenomena. Experience the terror of the Blitz. Concerts in the most unusual settings. Underground boat trips and hidden lakes. Ghost trails, vaults and witches walks. Gold mines, tin, copper, lead, flint and coal mines. Unbelievable tunnels and caves. Breathtaking and awe-inspiring subterranean places, many kept secret for countless years and all waiting to be discovered. Seeing is believing!

EXPERIENCE THE TERROR AND WONDER BENEATH YOUR FEET

book orders & suggestions ———————

We hope you have enjoyed reading this book and will want to purchase other titles in the series. Information on forthcoming titles not yet in print, together with details of any back issues available can be found on our website.

To place an advance order for a new title which will enable you to receive your copy prior to general public release, simply access our website and use the e-mail link to send us your full name, address and telephone number, together with the title of the book you wish to order. Payment is not required when placing your order. A secure direct telephone order line will be available in the near future.

We are always interested in hearing from our readers with any comments or suggestions. In particular, if you know of anything or any place that appears strange, unusual or simply bizarre to you, then please let us know.

e-mail direct:

bookorders@strangestbooks.co.uk
suggestions@strangestbooks.co.uk

or visit our website at:

http://www.strangestbooks.co.uk